James McGrath
IN A CLASS BY HIMSELF

BOOKS BY JONAH RASKIN

The Mythology of Imperialism

Out of the Whale

Homecoming

My Search for B. Traven

For the Hell of It: The Life and Times of Abbie Hoffman

More Poems, Better Poems

*Natives, Newcomers, Exiles, Fugitives: Northern
    California Writers and Their Work*

*American Scream: Allen Ginsberg's "Howl" and
    the Making of the Beat Generation*

*Field Days: A Year of Farming, Eating, and Drinking
    Wine in California*

Marijuanaland: Dispatches From an American War

Auras: New Poems

Rock and Roll Women: Portraits of a Generation

EDITED BY JONAH RASKIN

The Weather Eye

The Radical Jack London

CO-AUTHOR

Puerto Rico: The Flame of Resistance

James McGrath

IN A CLASS BY HIMSELF

The Life and Times of an
Extraordinary American Teacher,
Mentor, Cultural Ambassador,
and Pedagogical Pilgrim

Jonah Raskin

McCAA BOOKS
Santa Rosa, CA

ISBN 978-0-9838892-9-8
Library of Congress Control Number (LCCN) 2012940899

McCaa Books
1535 Farmers Lane #211
Santa Rosa, CA 95405-7535

www.mccaabooks.com

First published in 2012 by McCaa Books,
an imprint of McCaa Publications.

10 9 8 7 6 5 4 3 2 1

COLOPHON
Cover and page design by James Retherford. Composition by Hot
Digital Dog Design, Austin, TX. Text set in Century Schoolbook;
titles and subtitles in Memphis and Neue Helvetica Bold Condensed.
This book is printed on acid-free paper.

Contents

*To all the students
in all my classes
and to all my
colleagues, too.*

School Haiku: Take Out the "Sh" and It's Cool

BILL AYERS

Watching James McGrath
teach, listening to McGrath and his collaborators and
students reflect on the power of art and education, and
then reading this loving portrait woven so beautifully
together by Jonah Raskin is to hear the music that
both soothes and energizes. McGrath's teaching is by
turns disruptive and unruly, wild and straightforward,
always powered by love and joy and a yearning for justice, forever overflowing with life. I want to see more
and to hear more. I want to sing backup to that voice.

I'm reminded of Gwendolyn Brooks, winner of the
Pulitzer Prize for poetry in the early 1950s and poet
laureate of Illinois for many years, who asks in the first
line of her poem, "Dedication to Picasso," "Does man
love art?" She is standing in a large crowd of people
gathered in the plaza in downtown Chicago for the
unveiling of a giant sculpted bird/woman figure given
as a gift to the city by the iconic Pablo Picasso. She hur-

ries to answer her own question: "Man visits art," she writes, "but cringes / Art hurts / Art urges voyages."

Exactly! Art often begins in pain, horror, and uncertainty, but it inevitably opens to the immense territory of the possible. Art expands the horizons of the imaginable, standing beyond the world as such—the given or the received world—waving a colorful flag gesturing toward a world that should be or could be, but is not yet. If everything is perfect, if there is no need of repair or improvement, or if the world we have is none of our business, then we are inclined to banish the arts, cuff and gag the artists. They are a bother, agitators and activists urging voyages, explorations, questions, and queer company. If, on the other hand, we see ourselves as works-in-progress, born into a going world and catapulting through a vibrant history-in-the-making, and if we feel a responsibility to engage and participate, then the arts and the artists are the strongest allies we can have. It all depends on your angle of regard.

ii

Perhaps that's what Ferlinghetti was thinking when he published a slim volume with the provocative title *Poetry as Insurgent Art*, or what Picasso had in mind when he said, "Art is not chaste. Those ill prepared should be allowed no contact with art. Art is dangerous. If it is chaste, it is not art." Add to that Einstein's famous observation that "imagination is more important than knowledge. For knowledge is limited to all we now know and understand, while imagination embraces the entire world, and all there ever will be to know and understand." The poet, Ferlinghetti, meets the famous painter, Picasso, and the most renowned scientist of the century, Einstein, and they are immediately on the move and on the make, propulsive, dynamic, unsettled, and alive—on a voyage of discovery and surprise, up, up and

away, into the unknown. James McGrath finds himself
firmly in their exalted company: an artist/teacher urging voyages.

Much of what we call schooling today blinds us
to perspective and process and point-of-view, locks us
into the well-lit prisons of our linear ideas, forecloses
or shuts down or walls us off from options and alternatives, and from anything resembling meaningful
inquiry or relevant choice-making. Much of schooling
enacts a hollowed-out ethics and presents an unlovely
aesthetic. When schooling is based on obedience and
conformity, we are reminded that these qualities and
dispositions are the hallmarks of every authoritarian
regime throughout history. When schooling suppresses
the imagination, banishes the unpopular, squirms in the
presence of the unorthodox, and hides the unpleasant,
it becomes cowardly, dishonest, and immoral. We lose,
then, our capacity for skepticism, irreverence, doubt, and
imagination.

James McGrath offers a lifetime of alternatives, a
carpet bag filled with practical arts and concrete lessons
grounded in humanistic assumptions and democratic
dreams. He contradicts and disputes the dominant
metaphor in education today, which posits schools as
businesses, teachers as workers, students as products
and commodities. He re-ignites — and tries to live out
in his daily life — the basic proposition that all human
beings are of incalculable value and that life in a free
and democratic society is geared toward and powered
by a profoundly radical idea: the fullest development of
all human beings is the necessary condition for the full
development of each person; and, conversely, the fullest
development of each is necessary for the full development of all.

James McGrath foregrounds initiative, questioning, doubt, skepticism, courage, imagination, invention, and creativity—for him these are the central, not peripheral, ingredients of an adequate education. These are the qualities he models and nourishes, encourages and defends, and these qualities are precisely the precincts of the arts in their many incarnations. McGrath's concern is to help students ask questions, think the impossible, reinvent and refresh both themselves and their circumstances.

Foundational questions for free people are the vital stuff of McGrath's work: what's your story; how is it like or unlike the stories of others; what do we owe one another; what does it mean to be human; what qualities, dispositions, and knowledge are of most value to humanity; what kind of world could we reasonably hope to create; how might we begin?

iv

If we, along with our students, cannot reasonably ask these kinds of questions and then notice or invent alternatives, we are not free; if we cannot dwell in possibility, we are not fully alive. With McGrath we might become more mindful of the plea in Gwendolyn Brooks' "Boy Breaking Glass," "I shall create! / If not a note / a hole. If not an overture / a desecration." But I shall create—the fundamental and primal cry of the young and of every human being.

On the side of a liberating and humanizing education is a pedagogy of questioning, an approach that opens rather than closes the process of thinking, comparing, reasoning, perspective-taking, and dialogue. It demands something upending and revolutionary from students and teachers alike: Repudiate your place in the pecking order, it urges, remove that distorted, congenial mask of compliance: You must change! You can change your life!

You can change the world!

Haki Madhubuti, Gwendolyn Brooks' publisher, claims that art is a "prodigious and primary energy source" and then turns to the connection of art to education: "Children's active participation ... is what makes them whole, significantly human, secure in their own skin." He offers a kind of chant, each line ending with the words "with art" or "through art." Every teacher or student, parent or community member can play along and add on:

Magnify your children's mind with art!
Jump start their questions with art!
Keep their young minds running, jumping, and excited with art!
Keep them off drugs, respecting themselves and others, away from war with art!

This is the urgency, excitement, and energy that James McGrath generates and embodies.

Enter James McGrath

He ought to be famous, but he's only a teacher after all, and teachers are rarely famous in a country such as ours in which teachers are demonized and blamed by politicians for most if not all the ills of education. Maybe he will be famous on the day when America finally wakes up and realizes that teachers are "pilgrims to the horizon," to borrow a phrase that the African American author, Zora Neale Hurston, used to describe the mentors and instructors who helped to lift her out of her own prosaic life and to propel her into a strange and wonderful territory of learning and freedom. In these pages, I have lifted James McGrath—the focus of this book—out of the classroom and out of the schoolhouse and showed him off to the world. Or perhaps, I've invited the world into his universe to watch and listen to what he has done for most of his lifetime and what he still does.

Unwilling to wait for that future day when obscure and largely invisible teachers will be acknowledged, I've aimed to acknowledge him here and now.

James McGrath comes from a family without teachers and without degrees in higher education, but he was born to teach and nurtured to become a teacher, too, by his own teachers, who took him to distant horizons. When I first met him in 2008, he was eighty years old. He was teaching and enjoying it. Of course, by the time that most American teachers reach the age of eighty, they have long since retired. McGrath's age and his ability to survive and to thrive as a teacher at eighty, and then at eighty one, eighty two, and eighty three, impressed me, but his age was not the only factor that made him unique.

2

Soon after I met him, I learned that in his sixty-plus years of teaching, he had never been a specialist; he never taught just one grade, whether kindergarten, junior high, or the first year of college. He taught every grade, from pre-school to post-graduate school and almost every age from three to ninety nine. He was a science teacher and an art teacher, and he taught every aspect of art, worked in every medium, and all around the world, from the State of Washington to New Mexico and in Germany, France, Italy, Japan, Korea, the Philippines, and Okinawa. He taught in the Congo, Saudi Arabia, and Yemen—places on the map where Americans had never taught before and, if he brought American art around the world, he also brought home with him art from everywhere on the globe, except Antarctica. Wherever he worked he made teaching his art form, and he painted and sculpted, too, exhibiting his art in Europe, Africa, and the Americas. If he was forceful and outgoing, he was also quiet, moody, and introspective.

Just how much McGrath had meant to kids, teen-agers, and adolescents, I first learned from three former students. They studied with him at his first teaching job in the 1950s, and they all grew up to become renowned artists and art teachers themselves. Teachers are known by their own works, but they are also known by the works of their students, and this is especially true of McGrath and three particular students, Bill Wiley, Bob Hudson, and Bill Allan, whom I met before I met McGrath. When I sat down to talk with them, I was surprised to hear grown men talk with reverence and admiration about a high school art teacher who had helped to nurture them when they were teens. Fifty years later, they still remembered him and his classroom exercises, and they still called him McGrath or "Teach," not Jim or James. I met them at Bob Hudson's northern California house, which he and his wife Mavis Jukes have filled with art by friends such as Joan Brown as well as art that Hudson made with Wiley and Allan. Playful and funny, it's a testament to their friendship. At the dining room table at Bob's, there was wine, bread, cheese, and silence. Then Wiley jumped in and started the conversation.

3

"There's never been anyone like McGrath," he said. "There's just no getting away from him or his influence. He changed my life as an artist and as a teacher. At the University of California at Davis, where I taught for a decade, I wanted at first to turn my students into professional artists. As time went on I adopted the approach that McGrath used when we were at Columbia High School. I asked each and every student, 'What do you want to do?' and 'How can I help you get there?' I stopped trying to turn them into professional artists and instead urged them to be authentically themselves, which is what McGrath urged us to be."

Wiley added that McGrath wanted students to "mingle poetry, dance, music, painting." He encouraged Wiley to add words to his canvases and meld texts with colors and shapes. "McGrath persuaded me that there was more to drawing than making cartoons, which I loved to do almost all the time I was in high school," Wiley said. "He called this other thing 'art for art's sake,' and in 1953 in Richland, Washington, that was a bold, new idea."

Bill Allan offered a perspective of his own. "We had a vital student/teacher connection way back in Richland, Washington," he said. "Creativity went both ways and around and around. I think McGrath was influenced by us as much as we were influenced by him." Allan remembered that McGrath taught him that he didn't have to have a preconceived idea about art in order to make art. "His teaching helped me to become myself and trust myself," he said. "He brought me through a doorway."

Bob Hudson listened quietly. Then he began to talk, dredging up memories from his high school days. Hudson remembered that in 1954 McGrath taught him to drive a car and that they drove together to Seattle in a blizzard for an art exhibit—one of the first times that Hudson's work was in the public eye. They had adventures on the way to Seattle and on the way home, too, and Hudson said he'd never been the same since.

Now Wiley had another insight. "There was something of 'Mr. Rogers' about McGrath," he said. "He expressed the idea that you're good just the way you are and don't have to change anything about yourself. He was always authentic. He still is. I know he recently

4

turned eighty, but I think he's younger than all of us here combined."

Soon after that meeting with his former students, I met McGrath in person in Santa Fe and learned that he respected them as much as they respected him. "The arts captured Hudson, Wiley, and Allan at an early age, and they captured the arts," he told me. "Even as teenagers in high school at Columbia, they were like a garden of flowers blooming at its peak. They were not competitive with one another, and they were dedicated to art at the start, which was rare for young men in the 1950s. They came to class, and they got to work."

He paused for a minute as though searching for memories and added, "As a teacher and as a artist, I grew as they grew. We grew side-by-side in a community of learners that began in the classroom. All of us were part of a maturation process and a living, breathing struggle to be ourselves."

5

In the twenty-first century, teachers such as McGrath are rare, indeed. They have always been rare in any century. It's difficult though not impossible to find them today, and so this book is not only about a singular teacher but also about a way of teaching that now, for the most part, does not exist, not in America, Europe, or Asia. The loss, it seems to me, is ours, and so I have told McGrath's story hoping that students and teachers today will want to borrow his teaching methods and his teaching philosophy and bring his style into their own classrooms.

Neither I, nor McGrath, are partial to lists, and yet we know that lists can be helpful. Here, now in a gesture intended to open discussion rather than end it and at the start of a journey of discovery, are eleven teaching tips from James McGrath:

1. *Listen, empathize, and encourage.*
2. *Go on field trips.*
3. *Bring the outside world into the classroom.*
4. *Walk around your classroom; don't be tied to your desk.*
5. *Ask questions. Don't give away answers; help students find them for themselves.*
6. *Think the impossible. Do the impossible.*
7. *Take risks.*
8. *Keep moving; don't get stuck.*
9. *Simplify; less is often more.*
10. *Reinvent and refresh yourself.*
11. *Connect all the arts: music, dance, film, literature, and theater.*

CHAPTER ONE

Stutter Steps:
A Boy Becomes an Artist

I. Edison Elementary School

Long before he became a
pilgrim and led students to distant horizons, James
McGrath followed his own teachers on a pilgrimage that
began in boyhood. McGrath grew up in an era when
public schools were vital to neighborhoods, including his
own, and when schools and communities were linked by
students, teachers, parents, and administrators, too.

It was the Depression, and Americans might have
been depressed, but instead they felt a sense of hope
that, though social and economic conditions had thrown
them out of their jobs and homes, the world could be
changed for the better if people worked together. Education gave working class students such as McGrath a
sense of hope in the dark days of the Depression. His
own school provided food for thought for his family and
for the whole community, and the community provided
the school with a sense of identity. There were battles
and there was bitterness, but teachers, parents, and

even many of the kids believed in education and in democracy, and they knew that the two were linked.

McGrath was nearly six when he started school and already old enough to know the name of his street (South Prospect), the name of the school (Edison), and the name of his city (Tacoma). He knew the state was Washington and that the country was the United States of America. The president was Franklin D. Roosevelt. The year: 1934.

When the school year began, Jim sensed that he had already been formed by the routines of life at home: eating meals, going to sleep, waking, and starting all over again. Edison, his first school, was a strange place with strange sights, sounds, and smells, such as the harsh odor of the creosote-treated floors that was unlike anything at home. The school had big, unfamiliar, and yet wonderful rooms with new names: gymnasium and cafeteria.

8

If he had his way, he would rather be outdoors with the wind on his face as he ran or else sitting and watching a spider, fly, or bullfrog. He liked to play with friends in the woods and swamps on the outskirts of Tacoma, and he learned to enjoy solitude, too. His father taught him to carry a rifle, load and shoot, break it down and clean it. He could pull the trigger, too. More than hunting, however, he enjoyed picking wild blackberries with his mother, Millie May, who had attended Edison when she was a girl.

His dad, Francis McGrath, worked when he came home from his job, overalls covered with bits of plaster that fell to the living room floor. An artist and a craftsman, Francis was much in demand by people with new money building big houses. He was widely appreciated and handsomely rewarded for his creative plastering of the Temple Theater, one of the grand old movie houses in Tacoma, where Jim saw Saturday matinees and came to admire his dad's work. At home, he learned the lesson of hard work from both parents. "You got up early and went to work," he said. "You worked hard, and then you came home and worked some more."

At the same time that he started school, he developed a lisp and a stutter, and they came to define much of his identity. His speech therapy began at Edison Grade School, a red-brick building on the south side of Tacoma, where he was raised as an only child in an ramshackle house that his father renovated and where Jim had a room of his own. In the attic, he worked on his Mickey Mouse coloring book, adding reds, blues, and greens, and looked at the pictures in books such as James Fenimore Cooper's *The Deerslayer*. Sometimes he just roamed around the attic lost in thought.

He walked to school five days a week from his house at 5214 South Prospect. The walk covered ten blocks and to a six-year-old it felt like an epic journey. It took him past the houses of schoolmates, through a maze of streets, and across immense thoroughfares. First, second, and third grades were on the first floor of the school building; fourth, fifth, and six grades on the second flour at first seemed like a distant world, but before long he climbed the stairs and looked from the upper windows to the trees and the clouds on the horizon.

School got under his skin, and he came alive in the classroom under the gaze of teachers and in the company of schoolmates. He looked forward to books, homework, recess, and study hall. The unfolding universe of the school called to him, and he responded with his whole self. On special occasions, he went to school dressed as an Indian—revealing his own heartfelt secret identity, and, wearing a headdress, he posed for the school photograph meant for posterity.

A highlight of the day came in the afternoon when Miss Pakenham read aloud. An English teacher and a book lover, Pakenham kept the class entertained with passages from *Hitty*, Rachel Field's sad, funny story for children, which was published in 1929, a year after McGrath's birth, and which recounts the adventures of a doll. In social studies, students traced family histories, and Jim recounted tales he'd been told about his grandfather, a roving Irish sailor who abandoned his ship in Tacoma, met an American woman, and married her before disappearing into the wide world.

Jim listened to his classmates—Dick Chiarovano, Coral Venske, and Pat Playford—talk about their ancestors, a history lesson that taught him that all families weren't the same, but infinitely variable. One could learn from students as well as from teachers, he realized, and from the kids in his own neighborhood which was largely Irish, unlike the wealthier north side of Tacoma. The Boyles and the Sheets lived across the alley from the McGraths. The Irish families were large; there was always someone Jim's own age, such as Gardenia Rose Boyle, to play with.

Almost all of his teachers at Edison were women. It wasn't until he went to Robert Gray Junior High School that he met his first male instructor, Mr. Actor, who taught music. In 1934, all across America, grade school teachers were mostly women: young, old, married and unmarried, strict and easy-going.

At first, geography was Jim's favorite subject; he liked to collect rocks and look for fossils. Mrs. Mewhirter, who taught spelling, was a favorite teacher, and so he learned to spell correctly. Mewhirter also taught art; she handed out crayons, invited the students to draw,

10

and then to give titles to their work. Miss Nagley taught math. Lelia Russell, McGrath's speech therapist, gave him her undivided attention. In a small room on the first floor at Edison, Russell asked questions such as "How did you do in class today?" and "Who are your friends?" He struggled with words; some, like "vanilla," frustrated him more than others, and he simply didn't try. At the soda fountain in town, he asked for chocolate ice cream. He could say "chocolate" without stuttering.

Jim's aunts and uncles were among his first teachers. Aunt Margaret taught him to look at the world through the eyes of an artist and to see art in snail shells and raven droppings. Jim and Margaret went to Seattle to visit museums and to talk about the paintings they liked best and why. Outdoors, she taught him to sketch and paint with watercolors.

The man in the family who taught him the most was his uncle, Napoleon Bonaparte Bernier ("Nap" for short), a Chehalis Indian who lived with his wife, Sinnie, in a cabin without electricity or running water. Nap taught him how to read the signs of the natural world, how to hunt for agates—a rare and beautiful variety of quartz—how to talk to a skunk without getting skunked, and how to walk on a log floating in a river without falling off. Nap opened a portal that led to mountains, rivers, and an Indian way of existing on the face of the earth.

II. Going Beyond His Parents

After he graduated from Edison, he attended Robert Gray Junior High, located next to Edison. In seventh grade, he took an art class with Alice Jean Small and made posters. In Lotte Jellum's home economics class just for boys, he learned to cook. The real Aunt Jemima came to Edison on a whirlwind tour and encouraged Jim and all the students to eat a hearty breakfast.

At Lincoln High School, he wrote poems that emerged slowly, cautiously from his inner self. In one untitled work for Miss Cunningham's class that he wrote at the age of seventeen, he exclaimed, "These lines came to me as I / was trying best to sleep." In the poem, he describes the darkness of his bedroom and the "atmosphere of doubt." The poem ends hopefully, enthusiastically: "I heard a song—a chord—a note," he exclaims. "I knew it then! It was the world / of which a part is mine."

High school was on the far side of town; the streetcar took him there, and that journey was an adventure, too, but not as adventurous as high school itself. Ninth grade and then ten, eleven, and twelve divided him from his father, who read the daily newspaper but never sat down with a book, and from his mother, Millie, who kept house, cooked, crocheted, washed, and baked cookies. She didn't read either. No one in his immediate family had a high school diploma. No one had ever gone beyond eighth grade.

12

He studied French, which he loved, with Angele Messelin, whom he adored; he became the president of the French Club and thought he might become a French teacher, but his stuttering got in the way when he tried to pronounce simple sentences such as "Je m' appelle James McGrath." So he gave up French, but not the passion for learning and not the efforts to break his stuttering. He sang in the choir that was led by Margaret Goheen, who took the students to Fort Lewis—named after Meriwether Lewis of the Lewis and Clark expedition—to sing for the soldiers stationed there and on the verge of going off to war.

The summer after his junior year at Lincoln, he took a speech correction class with Dr. Lyman Partridge at Central Washington College of Education in Ellensburg, not far from Tacoma. Dr. Partridge had studied stuttering and was an expert, thanks to Charles Van Riper's influential books: *The Nature of Stuttering*, *The Treatment of Stuttering*, and *Speech Correction: Principles and Methods*. Charles Van Riper knew the subject intimately well from his own stuttering and empathized with stutterers.

Borrowing from Van Riper's methods, which emphasized exercises to reduce stress and anxiety, Dr. Partridge helped McGrath develop a sense of self-confidence, and that summer in Ellensburg he acted on stage in several campus plays and enrolled in a geology class with Professor George Beck, who led students on field trips to see fossils and petroglyphs.

13

"The summer of 1945 was life-changing," McGrath remembered. "I felt really free for the first time in my life, and I fell in love with college. In 1945, all of us, as a generation, came out from under the darkness of the war."

Back at home that fall, he told his parents that he wanted to become a geologist, and when he returned as a freshman to Central Washington College of Education (now Central Washington University), he majored in geology and set his sights on teaching geology. But as a budding geologist he was required to take college algebra; he earned a "D" and decided that geology wasn't meant for him.

Art looked more appealing. He took almost every art class that was offered: mechanical drawing, ceramics, creative design, lettering, murals, watercolors, modeling, sculpture, oil painting, weaving, and sketching. He enjoyed Sarah Spurgeon's art classes because she took students outside, invited them to look closely at trees, and then to draw what they saw. "It wasn't so much what you saw, but how you saw it," McGrath remembered. "Her drawing class was an education in looking, seeing, and noticing."

The class that matured him more than any other was Neil Koch's "Art and Modern Living" in which he listened to the music of Antonin Dvorak, Samuel Barber, and Igor Stravinsky. "Amazing!" he said to himself when he heard their work. Koch told him about the University of Oregon and encouraged him to apply and then to transfer when he was accepted. In 1948, at the age of twenty, and with a $1,500-a-year scholarship, McGrath moved from Ellensburg to Eugene.

14

The University of Oregon in Eugene was not at the hub of the American art world, but it had a thriving community of artists and educators, and McGrath responded to its vitality. In the Pacific Northwest, he recognized, there were Asian, European, and Native American traditions. The milieu was multicultural. Everything at the University of Oregon was bigger than anything at Ellensburg, and there were art exhibits and screenings of foreign films. McGrath still stuttered; he continued with speech therapy, saw that he made progress, and that progress encouraged him to continue. In Eugene, students who stuttered shared their feelings about stuttering, and so he learned that he wasn't a solitary stutterer.

In the School of Education at the University of Oregon, he listened to teachers talk about a wide array of lively topics: local control of schools, open classrooms, and the kinds of child-centered learning that educators would promote decades later. During his junior year, he majored in interior design, studied with Professor Brownell Fraser, and created a blueprint for an "ideal student space" in a new dormitory that was under construction on campus. From the School of Architecture, where he spent much of his time, he bounded to the Theater Department and painted the sets for Robert Ardrey's play *Thunder Rock* and Eugene O'Neill's *Marco Millions*. Among actors and directors, he came to appreciate the art of performance that would help him as a teacher who chose to make teaching his major art form.

On campus, he was very much a social animal. In fact, there was too much to do and see everyday and night of the week, and the variety of activities and disciplines made him dizzy. Still, he studied almost everything the institution offered, from architecture and aesthetics to zoology. At University High School in Eugene, he enjoyed "practice teaching" and in classrooms realized how he would feel as a full-time instructor. By the end of his time in Eugene, he had real world experience, a B.S., and a certificate in art education.

III. Glazer and Beall: Teachers and Mentors

In Eugene, two inspiring women turned his life around. Jean Glazer was a popular art professor. Paulette Beall was a charismatic mentor. Jean and Paulette both boosted McGrath's self-confidence and guided him gently through rough academic waters. When he looked back at his life, he would say that Paulette Beall "was the single most influential person in my life for more than fifty years. Always supportive, especially in dark times, she never said do this or do that. She never once told me what to do. Sometimes it seemed as though I was walking in her shoes, and sometimes it seemed as though she was walking in mine."

When Beall began to talk about art, her friends, her family members, and students stopped what they were doing and paid attention. In Oregon, newspaper reporters sought her for interviews and pithy quotations. Beall was messianic about art and elegiac about Picasso, Miró, Mondrian, Matisse, and Paul Klee. She asked most of the big questions, such as "What is Art?" and she talked about big topics such as "God, Man, and Space." Americans ought to be "awakened" to painting and taught its "specific language of line, form, and color," she insisted.

Born in France and thoroughly French, she complained about the horrid quality of the light in Eugene, Oregon: it was "far too dark, green, and heavy," she would say. The light in the south of France was her ideal. But she was open to new colors and new experiences, and her love of France and French didn't prevent her from adapting to Oregon. A docent at the Prince Campbell Museum of Asian Art in Eugene, she introduced McGrath to Asian art, and, under her spell, he broke away from the Eurocentric tradition that all of his other teachers praised.

Gentle and caring and with soft blue eyes, Beall could have lured him anywhere. In fact, she led him to the Willamette River in Eugene which she loved and he also came to love. From the start, she recognized something unique in him that wasn't apparent on the surface. "Do you write poetry?" she asked him on the first afternoon they met at the Campbell Museum of Asian Art. She had never seen McGrath before, but she sensed the soul of a poet. Their friendship grew from that beginning, and it grew, too, in an intuitive rather than a deliberate way.

"She was very philosophical," McGrath remembered. "She read Jacques Maritain, the French Catholic philosopher, and introduced me to the ideas in Maritain's seminal book, *Creative Intuition in Art and Poetry*, and especially to the idea of intuition. Beall looked to Asia, not to Europe, which was odd given the fact that she was a European. Soon after I met her, she took me to a room in the museum that housed statues of the Buddha—the first I had ever seen. 'This is where I come when I want quiet,' she said. After meeting her I came to appreciate tranquility."

Professor Jean Glazer stood at the opposite end of the philosophical spectrum from Beall. A graduate of the University of Chicago, she was a passionate intellectual and very Eurocentric. For years, she studied with László Moholy-Nagy, a Hungarian-born painter, photographer, and former professor at the Bauhaus school in Weimar, Germany. Glazer brought his ideas to Eugene where she urged her students to experiment in the arts.

17

"She believed in artistic exploration," McGrath said. "She told us to be alert to the process of creativity itself, to be aware of what the hand was doing, and what was happening in the heart. As you went along, you made discoveries. That was at the core of her philosophy."

In Glazer's classes, McGrath connected to the avant-garde movements of 1920s Europe. He embraced the work of Bauhaus founder Walter Gropius, the German-born architect who came to America in 1937 and designed school buildings and university centers using steel and glass. McGrath went back again and again to the Bauhaus to look for role models. "Like the Bauhaus, I, as a writer and instructor of human beings, want to teach inventiveness," he wrote in a paper for one of Glazer's seminars. He came to see the links between all the arts—painting, sculpture, photography, and film—and recognized that the arts were under the umbrella of something called "the media," a term just then beginning to find a wider audience than ever before in the wake of the communication revolution and the new media industries brought on by World War II.

IV. I Am a Stutterer

At the University of Oregon, he learned to appreciate improvisation, surrealism, Dada, James Joyce's stream-of-consciousness writing, Gertrude Stein's experiments with language, Paul Klee's whimsical art, and Piet Mondrian's abstract paintings. Modernism and then postmodernism swept him up and carried him away. When Merce Cunningham and John Cage came to Eugene, McGrath introduced himself and persuaded them to give him their autographs. They were living, breathing representatives of the avant-garde that he had read about in books and heard about in lectures.

He studied Herbert Read's *The Grass Roots of Art* (1946) and borrowed Read's concept of the "innocent eye of childhood." Read's work reinforced McGrath's faith in spontaneity, intuition, and craftsmanship—which he had first learned firsthand from his father. From Read—Sir Herbert after 1953, when Winston Churchill knighted him, despite his anarchism—McGrath learned to distrust teaching "imposed from without which is the command of a drill-sergeant." He delighted in Read's notion that in education "good results are produced apparently by no method at all, or by a system of hints and suggestions" that grew "out of the activity itself."

Synthesizing Glazer and Beall challenged every fiber in him, but he rose to the task. He even shocked Glaser in a paper he wrote for her teaching methods class. Entitled "Thoughts Toward a Child-Like Newness," it celebrated the vitality of children. One of the main goals of education, McGrath argued, was the "resurrection of the lost spirit of the child." To achieve that end, he explained, one had to have a "melting-togetherness of the soul and the spirit with the outer world."

Increasingly he wrote about his own stuttering and came out of the closet as a stutterer. "I am a stutterer," he wrote as though he had broken a barrier and had emerged far more whole than ever before. In an essay entitled "The Stutterer and Education," he explained that he had been urged not to become a teacher because he stuttered. "Why pick a profession that will only frustrate you and tire you," a teacher told him. "You'll only make nervous wrecks out of your students as well as yourself."

McGrath refused to give up his dream. He had to become a teacher. Moreover, he saw more clearly than ever before that his stuttering was a source of strength, not weakness. Stuttering was his wound, and, while it made him different, it also connected him to other people with wounds. Nearly everyone was wounded, he realized. He became adept at noticing wounds in others, even when they weren't on the surface, and he empathized with the wounded.

His parents noticed his new enthusiasm and urged him to become a teacher. They saw that by teaching he would be making something of himself, and they recognized his seriousness. In fact, he was serious enough to make inquiries about starting salaries, health plans, and retirement benefits. His head might have been in the clouds, but his feet were firmly planted in the practical work-a-day world.

After he received his B.S. degree, he enrolled in the Master of Science program at the University of Oregon and studied invertebrate zoology. In a graduate seminar, he compared art and science and argued that the creative processes in art were similar to the methods of inquiry used in the sciences.

He was in love with learning, teachers, and teaching. Now, too, he fell in love with Jean Livingston, a native of Portland, Oregon, and a fellow student whom he met on campus where she was learning to weave and make ceramics. On campus and off campus, walking and on picnics, dancing and romancing, they discovered that they shared a love of art, artists, and the theater. In

20

June 1951, after a brief engagement, they were married in an outdoor ceremony in Portland and drove off in a 1946 Chevrolet to Virginia City, Montana, where they joined the Virginia City Players, a professional theater company. The summer of 1951 was one long honeymoon. When he and Jean came back to the Northwest, James entered the Master of Fine Arts program at the University of Washington in Seattle and promptly met yet another mentor, Pauline Johnson, who taught art education crafts.

"Professor Johnson went to conferences and gave papers," McGrath said. "She was also down-to-earth. I learned a lot from her about the nuts and bolts of the classroom. I noticed that many teachers were anchored to their decks as though afraid that walking about the room might bring them into enemy territory. Pauline made the whole classroom her space; she walked around freely, looked at every student's work, and commented on it."

She, too, had a philosophy of education that McGrath found appealing. She didn't have pet students, and she didn't play favorites.

"Pauline valued everyone equally," he said. "It didn't matter whether you were an 'A' student or a 'C' student. No matter what, except for illness or a funeral in the family, you had to come to class, do the work, and participate. She let all of her students know that she cared and that she wanted us to succeed. That made a world of difference."

V. The Perfect Place to Begin to Teach

Before he could finish the M.F.A. program, McGrath was hired by Mr. P. A. Wright, the superintendent of schools in Richland, Washington. Wright met McGrath on campus and, impressed by his hands-on skills, persuaded him to join the faculty at Columbia High School. "At the University of Washington, I worked as a pressman for the campus newspaper," McGrath explained. "The day I met Wright, I was wearing overalls covered with ink and looked more like a tradesman than a college student. That appearance worked in my favor. Wright could see that I wasn't afraid to roll up my sleeves and get dirty. It was clear to him I wasn't an artsy bohemian."

In high desert country, Richland was just what he wanted. "I really could not have asked for any place better than Richland," he said. "It was the perfect place to start teaching." When McGrath arrived for work at Columbia High School the first day of the fall semester in September 1953, he still stuttered. But he stopped stuttering that first day. All the years of speech therapy finally paid off. "I remember looking out at the students at Columbia High School," McGrath said. "They seemed bright, eager, and restless. I knew that if I was going to instruct them and if they were to learn, I would have to exercise control. That meant not stuttering."

John Haugse—who graduated from Columbia and went on to teach at Harvard—remembered his first day in McGrath's class. "I was aware that he wasn't much older than we were," Haugse said. "He stood there at the front of about thirty students and when he started to stutter I thought, 'Oh no, this is going to be awful.' But by the end of the class that feeling was gone. I was con-vinced—most of us were—that his classroom was the right time and the right place for us to be. Nearly all of the teachers didn't listen to us. Now, suddenly here was a teacher who listened, empathized, and encouraged us. Because of that he came to seem larger than life."

In 1952, at the age of twenty four, McGrath wasn't much older than the students, and in the hallways he was occasionally mistaken for a student. In the class-room, however, he was clearly in charge and usually transparent about almost everything he did. "He is always Mr. McGrath," one student wrote in an essay about him. She added, "He never goes out of his way to impress anyone."

CHAPTER TWO

The Bomb and the River: High School Art

I. The Crisis in Education

Johnny couldn't read. Jane couldn't read either. Or so their parents and teachers complained. In the 1950s, Rudolf Flesch—the best-selling Austrian-born American author—noticed a sharp decline in literacy among students and wrote a provocative book about the subject entitled *Why Johnny Can't Read—and What You Can Do About It* (1955) that shook up educators.

In the 1950s, and especially after the Russians launched their satellite, Sputnik, no one who was concerned about children failed to notice what came to be called "the crisis in education." The phrase was widely used, though the German-born intellectual, Hannah Arendt, defined it more clearly than anyone else in an essay entitled "The Crisis in Education." McGrath experienced the crisis firsthand and, with his fellow teachers, tried to understand it. If students didn't read or couldn't read, the teachers at Columbia High School wanted to know why and what they could do to make reading exciting for John Haugse, Bill Allan, Bob Hudson, Bill Wiley, and their classmates.

For McGrath, the crisis in education went beyond the classroom and reflected the crisis in the society itself. Problems at school, he told colleagues, mirrored the problems of the world-at-large. A generation of young Americans had come of age during the Depression and World War II, and, in many cases, as McGrath recognized, they were deprived of the experiences of childhood. Uprooted by economic crisis and war and then shocked by the blasts of the atomic bomb, they often lacked roots in a community and were denied family ties, despite the talk of "togetherness" and the TV shows that depicted happy nuclear families.

Many of the students lacked nurturing parents, and so McGrath became father, mother, older brother, confidant, as well as teacher, mentor, and more. His job called for all those roles, though they weren't written into his job description. He also worked as custodian, cleaning up the classroom that was a mess after students made art. He was a kind of preacher, too, who presented students with guidelines about right and wrong and a therapist to whom troubled students turned.

Ivan Illich—the Viennese-born student of theology—would complain in *Deschooling Society* (1971) about authority figures in the classroom. Illich argued that teachers held far too much power in their hands, and he urged decentralized power and "deschooling" by which he meant ending the role of the school as an enforcer of the dominant paradigm. "School is the advertising agency which makes you believe that you need the society as it is," he wrote. McGrath allowed that Illich's way was one way, though not the only way, of looking at the relationship between the school and society. He argued that Illich omitted all that was positive about school and failed to appreciate the many diverse roles that underpaid teachers had to play in the classroom to create a semblance of order for genuine learning to take place. "There was no one but me to clean up, no one else the students could turn to for help, and no one who could offer them guidelines," McGrath said. "I know that I had power, and I know that power corrupts, but we also diffused power in the classroom. Students such as Bill Allan took on some of the roles that I might have played. Allan and others presided over panel discussions about the arts which we held at Columbia."

Moreover, the whole school aimed for a kind of "de-schooling." One day a year—"Mad Day"—Columbia was "in the hands of the seniors." On Mad Day, they acted as teachers and administrators so that they could understand how the school worked and appreciate "dynamic citizenship." Granted, it was only a symbolic shift of power, but Mad Day generated a sense of responsibility that lasted for much of the semester. Once the students tasted the roles of teachers and administrators, they didn't forget them.

25

II. Nuclear Culture

At the start of his teaching career, McGrath wanted to make students aware of the old and the new. In a history class, for example, he invited students to travel back in time. He pointed out that "creative artists" had lived in what came to be called the State of Washington more than ten thousand years before Columbus's 1492 arrival in the New World.

"The truly modern or contemporary artist, like the truly modern scientist, must always be an innovator, pathfinder, seer," he told Wiley, Hudson, Allan, and others in a class on the place of the artist in the twentieth century.

McGrath wasn't afraid to use the word "must." He told students that they "must be creative-minded and must free themselves from all clichés." They "must" also learn, he explained, to appreciate the artistic potential in "found objects" such as tin cans, broken jars, and garbage. He counted on students to attend classes, be punctual and courteous, respect the property of others, and cooperate. McGrath insisted that all students had to communicate with one another and with him. He assigned term papers, insisting they "must be original." He gave no one grades, he explained. Students earned them. Practically anyone could earn a "C," he explained; "A's" were harder. Students had to do "more than what is expected" for an "A." As for "F's"—"Never had a student sunk that low," he explained.

When they broke rules, he let them know he was disappointed. "When you are gone from the building, it's dead," he told students after an egregious spate of absences. On another occasion, when students didn't take an exam seriously, he was so angry that he wrote out and delivered word-for-word a talk entitled "I Am Going to Get Personal." He poked fun at and prodded students who thought, "I'm me and I should get an A," and at others who had the attitude that "a girlfriend is the biggest thing, money is God, and a job after school is it."

Students surrounded McGrath all day long whether on school ground or in his own house. There were kids, kids, and more kids in every family in Richland, though they often lived in worlds of their own making and often apart from their parents. Richland was a paradise for kids and for many of its citizens, too. The streets were clean, the neighborhoods were quiet, the houses new and often prefabricated. The place had the feeling of a hastily constructed experimental laboratory on the very edge of the world. In the 1950s, Richland was said to have had the largest trailer park in the United States. Like most towns, it had a fire department, movie theaters, the Rotary and the Lions, as well as Parent Teacher Associations. Businessmen joined the Chamber of Commerce. Students belonged to Future Homemakers of America. There were homecoming queens, cheerleaders, and captains of teams.

Still, there was no other town anywhere quite like Richland. It was mostly white and largely Protestant, but it was more than that. Indeed, Richland might have provided the perfect setting for a science fiction movie about mad scientists and weird aliens who take over everyone and turn them into zombies. Richland was a boomtown, a company town, and a government town, all in one. Designed by the Army Corps of Engineers, it was laid out like a perfect grid with streets named after soldiers and scientists as though all that mattered was war and science. During the whole time that McGrath lived and worked there, it was under the jurisdiction of the Atomic Energy Commission; General Electric ran the town day-in and day-out. It was a bizarre place in a bizarre time.

In the 1950s, of course, the atomic bomb occupied the thoughts of most Americans. Richland had a curious affinity to the nuclear age that it advertised and promoted. At Columbia High School, the athletic teams were "the Bombers." The school mascot was a "bomb"—make-believe, of course—placed on the basketball court at halftime. The school icon was the mushroom cloud that formed in the atmosphere after the detonation of atomic bomb blasts. Richland celebrated "Atomic Frontier Days"—a nuclear age fair and carnival with carousels, merry-go-rounds, popcorn, and hotdogs.

There was good reason for the fixation on the bomb. In Hanford—a factory town fifteen miles north of Richland—plutonium was manufactured behind high fences and thick walls. Hanford plutonium was used in the atomic explosion, code name "Trinity," that took place on July 16, 1945, in New Mexico. It also was used in the bomb—known as "Fat Man"—that was dropped on Nagasaki, Japan, in 1945. Hanford provided a key nuclear link in "The Manhattan Project," and Richland was Hanford's link to the real world. Even the makers of bombs had to go home and sleep at night. Immediately after the end of World War II, the production of plutonium stopped. Then, as the Cold War heated up, Hanford went back to the business of making bombs. McGrath arrived in Richland at the start of the bomb boom and the peculiar way of life that accompanied it.

Men (and a small number of women) worked at Hanford and ate, slept, and watched TV with their families in Richland. The fathers of most of McGrath's students, including Hudson's and Wiley's, worked at Hanford. They disappeared in the morning and reappeared in the evening, their lips sealed about everything they'd seen, heard, and made with their own hands. Nearly everything was top secret; almost all information was classified, and everyone who worked there had to have clearance. For years, McGrath had no clear idea what went on at Hanford.

In and around Richland, it was difficult to know

when and where government space ended and private space began. Granted, one could decorate one's home, lock the doors, and draw the curtains to ensure a modicum of privacy, but in the 1950s the houses were government-owned and so was the furniture. Moreover, residents had an uncanny feeling they were watched—and, indeed, they were. Students encountered the security forces that protected Hanford. Sent out of the classroom and into the desert to draw, young budding art students such as Allan and Wiley were stopped and questioned by the police. Bill Witherup was one of the first students to grasp the vast underground network that existed all across Richland.

Witherup—the first editor of the yearbook under McGrath's supervision—was a creative student who went on to become a creative adult. He graduated in 1953, became a writer, studied with the poet Theodore Roethke, and drew inspiration for his own work from his years in Richland. The bomb cast a long shadow on Witherup's life, and in *Men at Work*, a collection of his poems and essays, he explored it and mapped it. He described his father's secret work at Hanford, and he described the men who worked for Military Intelligence—known as MI—who called on his parents to make sure they weren't stealing government secrets— and perhaps for the sake of pure intimidation, too.

29

The spying and the secrecy affected everyone. They affected the schools, the teachers, the students, and their parents, almost of them newcomers who had flocked to Richland to find work. Many students had not grown up in a community, and many of them had no ties to any church, civil group, or institution. They were in need of a guide and a mentor, and McGrath did his best to perform those roles for Bill Witherup, Bob Hudson, Bill

Allan, William Wiley, and their classmates.

Born in 1937, Bob Hudson bounded about the West with his parents, who looked for work all through the 1940s until they arrived in Richland. The tiny trailer in which they lived after they settled down was too small to accommodate both Bob and his parents, so he slept in their 1937 Ford in winter and outdoors under the stars in summer.

"The trailer was cramped with no place for me to have privacy," he remembered. "I camped out all through high school." What gave Hudson a sense of belonging was the art he made. "I was drawing by the time I was eight," he said. "I would have flunked out of schools all over the West if it hadn't been for art."

Like Hudson, Wiley also bounced about with his parents: from Indiana to Texas, California, and Washington. Art wrapped a cocoon around him and gave him a sense of privacy. "When we traveled around, I read books and did art work in the backseat of the family car," Wiley remembered. "I made whole towns out of cardboard, and I put into my art everything that I saw from the back seat: goofy road signs and billboards, too, that made their way into the cartoons I did as a kid and then as a student in McGrath's art classes."

Dorothy Dowis arrived in Richland at the age of eight and lived there until she graduated from high school. "Richland was a strange place," she remembered. "It was insular, anonymous, and conformist. Everything was compartmentalized. People were patriotic and proud of the fact that the plutonium for 'Fat Man' had been manufactured at Hanford. I came to see the place as one big B. F. Skinner experiment. McGrath was everything that Richland was not, and it's amazing that he taught there."

30

III. Subverting the Dominant Paradigm

McGrath offered an alternative to the way of life
that dominated Richland. The word "counterculture"
didn't exist then, but his was a countercultural way of
thinking and being in the world. To his students, he
was very different from nearly everyone else at school
and in the community, and they were drawn to him,
though he was not the first good teacher they knew.
Thelma Pierson, an art teacher in the local junior high
school, had shown them what good instruction could be.
McGrath built on the foundations she provided and then
took her former students into realms where they had
not ventured before.

"Good teachers build on other good teachers, even
if they never meet or see one another," McGrath said.
"Students carry them from grade to grade and so there's
real continuity."

What McGrath did and how he did it was different
from most other teachers, and, in his role as pilgrim
to the horizon, he attracted his first band of followers.
Some parents were downright leery of him. Donna Mac-
Gregor's parents thought that he was trying to create a
cult and to cast himself as the cult leader. Still, others
appreciated what he was doing.

"There was a curious bond between my mother and
McGrath," John Haugse remembered. "My father was
an authoritarian, and he was suffocating me. My mother
saw that McGrath's instruction brought me away from
the kind of fearful, judgmental things that my father
practiced in our house."

McGrath reached out to the parents of his students.
He belonged to the Richland Art Association and went
to art exhibits, where many of the local artists were also

the mothers of his students and where they could chat.
Report cards were another link. Of course, McGrath
filled in grades in the space allocated. He also used
every inch on the report cards to write lengthy comments in very small letters.

In every way he could, he took students away from
fear, force, and punishment. Dorothy Dowis explained:
"I was already eighteen when I walked into his classroom, but his was the first non-fear-based teaching that
I ever experienced. It was 1953, and in those days there
was a huge chasm between children and adults, though
not with McGrath. He had interesting visuals on bulletin boards, and he included everything: painting, dance,
theater, poetry, music, and sculpture. He also taught all
kinds of media."

32 McGrath played music and showed films. Charlie
Chaplin was a favorite, along with documentaries about
Alexander Calder, Mark Tobey, and Navajo music. At
the end of the year, he gave tests—multiple choice and
true/false—but for the most part students didn't have to
"regurgitate things," as Dorothy Dowis put it. "We had
to write how we felt about something," she remembered.
There were student-run panel discussions, too, on topics such as "The Responsibilities and the Opportunities
of the Contemporary Artist" that Bill Allan helped to
moderate.

McGrath took the students away from the world of
the bomb into the world of nature, and especially to the
banks of the Columbia River and the vast stretches of
the desert.

"He was subverting the dominant paradigm in the
Cold War," Bill Witherup remembered. "He wasn't the
man in the button-down shirt or any kind of uniform,
and he bespoke a gentleness that enabled us to recognize

the rigidity of the culture."

Field trips were an essential part of McGrath's teaching repertoire. Almost every year, the culminating experience for the class was a trip to Celilo Falls, a traditional tribal area on the Columbia River where the Indians built and launched platforms that they used for fishing.

"Before McGrath came to Richland, I didn't know there were Indians in the area," Dorothy Dowis said. "I didn't know much about the river, and I also had never heard anyone say the desert was beautiful until McGrath did. People denigrated it as a wasteland of sage brush and sand. I had always thought it was beautiful but was afraid to say so."

At school, life was good. At home, it was bad, and it went downhill fast. Even the students saw that McGrath's marriage to his wife, Jean, was coming apart, and that, as one student wrote, "He often unintentionally neglects his home life." They learned to avoid him when his moods were dark, but he learned to use them creatively as a classroom teacher and as an artist. Despite the crisis in education and in his own marriage, McGrath invented himself as an art teacher at Columbia. During the three years that he taught there, from 1952-1955, he learned from the students and by making his own art, too. He would explore a subject—printmaking or painting with oils or watercolors, for example—and learn it so thoroughly that he could teach it almost without having to think about it. Not everything worked or was successful, however, though he and the students learned to learn from mistakes. Turning a tall telephone pole into a totem pole proved to be impossible; the chemically treated pole had to be dragged out the same way it had been dragged in, with a great deal of huffing and puffing.

Of course, McGrath was new to teaching at Columbia High School, and that newness enabled him to look for new horizons and find his own way. "I had new eyes," he remembered. "I didn't have many preconceptions, and that was useful as a beginner." His classroom was almost brand new, too, with new desks and chairs. For the most part, he had top-quality supplies: paper, brushes, paints, and clay, but he also brought his own materials for weaving and sculpting. Mostly, he had academic freedom to teach the way he wanted to teach without interference.

McGrath served as the faculty adviser to the yearbook which, with ample funding from the school, became a work of art widely praised for its elegance and originality. He broke the rules for high school yearbooks and yet maintained the highest of standards; one issue boasted a burlap cover that had faculty members and parents wondering if experimentation hadn't gone too far. But the students loved the ground-breaking approach to an activity long bound by tradition.

McGrath's model for the Columbia yearbook was *Flair* magazine, published in Paris and London and edited by Fleur Cowles, who also worked for *Look* magazine. There were holes in the cover of *Flair* and cutouts on selected pages. The first issue, which came out in February 1950, featured fiction by Tennessee Williams and artwork by Lucian Freud. The ads were artistic, the colors spectacular, and the students on the yearbook staff were excited to use *Flair* as a template. Cowles was flattered by the homage to her magazine and wrote to the students—and McGrath—to tell them how pleased she was to hold their work in her hands.

IV. Big and Small, Rocks and Indians

McGrath's biggest coup as the adviser to the yearbook was to persuade Frank Lloyd Wright to write
an essay for it. Publication of the essay made James
even more controversial than he had been. Soon after
he started to teach in Richland, he uttered the word
"damn," and a student reported him to the principal.
He was told never to use the word "damn" again. Frank
Lloyd Wright's essay was more provocative than "damn."
It was plainly subversive in 1955 when Wright was
eighty six years old and famous as an innovative architect. He would die four years later, in 1959; he had no
reason to hold back.

It made perfect sense for McGrath to ask him to
contribute an essay for the yearbook. The school was
planning to construct a building on campus, and, from
McGrath's point of view, Wright was at the top of the list
of the best architects in America. Wright's essay for the
yearbook was hardly balanced. In fact, it sounded like
the parting salvo of a man who had been at war with
American values for much of his life. Students, teachers,
and parents could read his provocative comments about
the country's "contented wage-slaves" and about "the
cash-and-carry system," which he insisted had taken
over the whole economy. McGrath might as well have
invited Karl Marx or his anarchist hero, Herbert Read,
to write an essay for the yearbook.

Wright was against everything "big," including big
schools. "The big anything is becoming more and more
a self-defeating institution," Wright complained. He
advocated decentralization, democracy, and "individual
responsibility in freedom." He wanted small classrooms,
as small as was feasible without undoing the function of

35

the school. The new building at Columbia and "all buildings universally," Wright argued, should be "adapted to the uses of the young life growing up there." He wanted trees, flower beds, and vegetable gardens that the students would cultivate themselves. It was essential, in his view, to be close to nature where students would discover "the mysteries of the soil." The mysteries of the atom were unimportant to him, and big weapons, such the atomic bomb, were in his view as self-defeating as big buildings. Moreover, in the society of the future, Wright wrote, the most important members of the community, and the highest paid, would not be generals or heads of corporations, but teachers.

The yearbooks for 1954 and 1955 were among McGrath's major achievements at Columbia. They reflect his art and philosophy, and they show how the surrounding environments—the sands of the desert and the waters of the Yakima and Columbia rivers—influenced the students. Wiley, Hudson, and Allan did some of their best work as high school students on the staff of the yearbooks.

Nearly as lasting as the yearbooks were the meetings the students had with the Yakima tribe—who lived along the river and who offered a window into a way of life close to the earth without roads, dams, and hydroelectric power. McGrath's students met the Yakima and their chief, Wilson Charley, at the river. Charley also came to McGrath's classroom and talked to the students about tribal rites, rituals, and ancient attachments to the earth.

Along the banks of the river, students observed the Indians as they caught, smoked, and ate salmon. They watched as the Indians drummed and danced around bonfires in the darkness of the night. Back at school, they drew ancient Indian symbols and signs and included Indian drums and feathers in their art. Bill Allan loved the days and the nights along the river. Hudson remembered the smoke, the salmon, and the storytelling. Wiley found the Indian singing, dancing, and drumming emotionally moving.

Almost every week, McGrath sent students out of the school to look, see, notice, and listen. He awakened their eyes, ears, and their sense of touch. The assignments and the exercises he gave the students challenged them, and they would remember them for the rest of their lives. For one class, McGrath invited the students to go to the Columbia River, find a small stone, carry it all day, and then write about it. The students were to "relate the discoveries they made about their stone," and they were to describe in words "the feelings about the stone and what the stone has been doing."

Twenty one students leaped at the opportunity, including James Scoggin, who wrote what was perhaps the most creative essay in the class and which ended, "I am not finished!!!"—a common complaint of students who raced against deadlines. "My rock is a rough and ragged individual," Scoggin wrote. "I suppose all rocks are wise to a certain degree, but mine had a high IQ to start with. The rock doesn't yet trust me. My rock is an introvert. It could over time grow into my friend."

V. Flow

McGrath spent so much time at school and in school-related activities that he was rarely at home with his wife and daughters. The crisis at home intensified year after year, and his marriage fell apart. Deeply troubled, he wanted to do the right thing, and he thought that if he moved to another place and started teaching anew, he might be able to reconnect to Jean and save his marriage. So he applied to teach in Germany at a school under the jurisdiction of the U.S. Army for the dependents of American servicemen and women. He was hired immediately, and Jean and the girls packed their bags, said goodbye to family members and friends, and began to make plans to see Paris and the Rivera.

In 1955, on the eve of his departure from Richland, McGrath offered a few parting words to the students. The theme of his last talk was "Flow," and he connected it to the Columbia and to all rivers. "Be a river for a time," he told Allan, Wiley, Hudson, Scoggin, Dowis, Mankowski, MacGregor, and the others. "Make your life your art. Find your gait of living. Look for the goodness in a child."

CHAPTER THREE

Breaking Down
and Building Up

I. An American in Paris

In Vincente Minnelli's 1951
movie, *An American in Paris*, Gene Kelly plays Jerry
Mulligan, a G.I. from New Jersey who won't go home
at the end of World War II and who wants to become
an artist. If McGrath needed a role model, Mulligan
provided one; *An American in Paris* reinforced his own
dream of making art in Paris and living on the Left
Bank among American expatriates and French artists.
Minnelli's picture came out just as the New York art
world, riding on the crest of abstract expressionism,
crowned itself the new cultural capital of the world.
The crowning was premature. In fact, in the 1950s,
Paris still buzzed with innovative American and European artists. Jean Dubuffet and Alberto Giacometti
continued to work in Paris, and American artists such
as Sam Francis skipped New York altogether to paint
in Europe. Rumors of the death of Paris as an art capital were greatly exaggerated; Paris continued to pull

writers and artists into its orbit.

In 1955, at the age of twenty seven, McGrath wanted, more than anything else in the world, to be an artist on the Left Bank. Jerry Mulligan might have spoken for him when he says, "I'm a painter. That's all I ever wanted to be." Granted, McGrath wasn't as single-minded as Mulligan. He was a painter and determined to paint, but painting wasn't the only thing he wanted to do. He also wanted to teach. He wanted to teach and to paint, and at times it wasn't clear to him what came first. Like Jerry Mulligan, he was pulled in several different directions.

"I wanted to be in Daniel Cordier's gallery in Paris. I wanted to be like Sam Francis," McGrath remembered. But he also wanted to meet the demands and needs of his family. "Can I do everything?" he wondered. "Can I paint, teach, be a devoted husband and a caring father? Or will something have to give?"

II. INTUACTION

As far back as the 1940s, Paris had tugged at McGrath. It went on tugging at him from the moment he landed in Europe, and it wouldn't stop. He went to Paris and saw artwork by Louise Nevelson—the Russian-born sculptor who came to the United States in 1905—and by Sam Francis—the California-born painter and ex-G.I. who might have been the inspiration for Jerry Mulligan. McGrath drove to Bern for an exhibit of Klee and to Venice where a fellow American teacher, Jennie Lea, introduced him to Peggy Guggenheim, the legendary American patron of the arts. In Venice, for the first time, he saw Jackson Pollock's work—hanging in Guggenheim's bathroom—and he appreciated Pollock's daring.

For much of the time he lived in Europe, he asked himself, "What makes American art different from European art"? "What are its unique sources and strengths"? And "Where is it headed"? Soon he would see signs of the future of art in New York. German friends introduced him to the work of two American artists, Robert Rauschenberg and Jasper Johns, and, on a brief trip to the U.S., he visited Rauschenberg and Johns in their studio. There was polite conversation and tea and then Rauschenberg rolled out a new piece he had just finished—a goat on wheels with a tire around its neck. Johns showed McGrath a new painting—an all-white American flag.

In Germany, McGrath taught in the U.S. Army schools that served the sons and daughters of soldiers stationed in Europe. Some parents also worked for American companies and came from corporate cultures as rigid as the military. In the 1950s, American troops were stationed all over Europe, and so the schools for the children of those soldiers were all across Europe too. The bases were isolated islands of America in a sea of European culture. The schools, K-12, were meant, of course, to provide students with the basics of reading, writing, and arithmetic. They also aimed to remind students that, though they were living in Europe, they were Americans, and so classes imbued them with a sense of American history and values.

McGrath wanted the students to appreciate European traditions, customs, and languages, too, and he designed the curriculum to bring Europe into their consciousness. Helped by the fact that one of the leading pedagogical buzzwords of the day was "intercultural," he aimed to connect American and European cultures. He dove head first into European culture, bringing students along with him as often as possible on jaunts to museums, book fairs, churches, and castles. What he aimed to do was to show students that there were alternatives to the drill and the drone of military life.

McGrath's first year of teaching in Germany did not live up to his expectations, though he met a more ethnically diverse student body than in white Richland. American soldiers were black and Hispanic, as well as white, and so were their children. Moreover, many kids were just learning to read and write and to adjust for the first time to life away from parents. Before he arrived in Germany, McGrath had never taught young children or boys and girls in their early teens. Now interacting with thirteen- and fourteen-year-olds, he was prompted to think, write, and talk about adolescence.

To call a person "an adolescent" was often "pejorative," he observed. It need not be, he concluded. "Adolescence," he told American schoolteachers in Germany, was "a time of expectancy, hope, and adventure." It was a good time to reach young people through the arts, because the arts offered "visual proof" that students were learning and "forming critical judgments" when tests often failed to assess growth and development.

In Frankfurt, Germany, as in Richland, he sent students outdoors to sketch, urging them to "wander around," not be bound by "the literal," and not get into too much trouble, either. He emphasized the importance of background and foreground, colors, shapes, and textures, and he invited students to "tell the old story in a new way." He also urged his fellow teachers to send their students into Frankfurt, and he discovered that American students in Europe were often more aware of Europe than their own parents. When they painted, sketched, and drew, they offered tangible evidence of the ways that Europe had registered on their own inner worlds. Moreover, for the students whose families had come from Europe, living in Europe provided an opportunity to discover their roots. The continent was a seedbed of ideas, images, art, and history.

In every grade, what was important, McGrath said, was intuition and spontaneity. In the mid-1950s, he coined the word "INTUACTION," which he capitalized, to convey the idea that teachers ought to move quickly in classroom settings. Prolonged thought and delayed responses had their limitations; ideas became stale, though acting on intuition alone, he realized, was insufficient. Indeed, he wanted a balance between planning and spontaneity.

Some of the overarching ideas that he developed about education, while he was in Germany, are evident in the guidelines he wrote about bulletin boards which, he insisted, had to "catch the eye" and persuade adolescent boys and girls to notice what was happening to their bodies, their heads, and in Germany, too. Making a bulletin board was "a giving and a taking, a building up and a tearing down," he explained.

The notion of art as a process of construction, deconstruction, and reconstruction—which he came to appreciate in the ruins of post-World War II Europe—marked an advance in his own thinking and influenced his own art and his teaching.

After his first year of teaching in Europe, McGrath evaluated himself and his methods. He decided that the main purpose of an art education was to make the young "aware of their worth as creative citizens of the world." Some students, he concluded, would grow up to become artists, but he insisted, "we do not teach them to be artists." As a teacher, he wanted to create environments in which students could, on their own, "discover a way to express their feelings about the world."

He felt better suited for high school than junior high, and, from the start, he sent the American high school kids into the oldest part of Frankfurt, away from the military base where most of them lived with their parents, and urged them to break away from "preconceived concepts and practices." He gave them pens, brushes, and ink and directed their attention to Frankfurt's *strassenbahn* (the streetcars), the Eschenheim (the city's landmark tower), and the Palmengarten (a nineteenth-century botanical garden.)

In December, he took students to the Christmas market and the annual book fair that brought publishers, editors, and writers from around the world. He persuaded Heine Heckroth—who won an Academy Award for his work on the film, *The Red Shoes*—to give a presentation entitled "What's So Special About Special Effects?"

Germany spurred McGrath's creativity. He painted every minute he could find, and he launched a one-man show at the Zimmergalerie Franck in Frankfurt in 1956 when he was twenty eight years old. Granted, the Zimmergalerie Franck wasn't Paris, but it added confidence. Moreover, it was through his art that he made new friends such as Toni Drees, the daughter of an aristocratic German family who lost much of their wealth to the Nazis. Frau Drees held an annual party—a *faschingsfest*—with wine, food, and costumes. The Germans weren't exactly wild, but they could be unconventional, McGrath discovered. Among them he felt freer than ever before. He went to the Jazzkeller in Frankfurt to hear American and European musicians, and he learned enough German to be able to carry on conversations and even make puns.

The conflict between the freewheeling artist and the family man came to a head when he was offered a position as an art teacher at the American High School in Paris. At first, it seemed too good to be true; he could teach and at the same time he could paint in Paris, of all places. The idea appealed to Jean and to the girls, too. They could become Parisians.

Then McGrath was offered another position — as art director for all of the American schools in Germany, France, Italy, and Ethiopia. As the art director, he would have the opportunity to travel freely across Europe and influence the teaching of art in four countries. Wanderlust seized hold of him. The title of "art director" tantalized him, and he accepted the position. Then, at the end of the school year, the whole family — Jean, James, and the girls — packed up and went home for summer vacation. James rented a house in Portland and then returned to Europe, expecting that Jean and the girls would join him after he found an apartment for all of them to live together. They never did return. Once she was settled in Portland, Jean filed for divorce on the grounds that her husband had deserted her.

45

"It was true. I had deserted her," McGrath remembered. "It hurt to lose my family. On the other hand, I had the freedom that I had dreamed of having." There was no point going back to Oregon, no point negotiating with Jean once again. He had done all he could do. It was time to move on, to be independent, live fully and not try to do things by halves.

He settled into his new job as art director for all

the American schools in Germany, France, Italy, and
Ethiopia. He lived in the Bachelor Officer's Quarters—
he had the rank of lieutenant—but for three or four
weeks at a time he was a roving American in a VW
bus loaded with pens, inks, paints, and papers that he
distributed to teachers and students all over the continent. Even Jerry Mulligan would probably have envied
McGrath's new life.

CHAPTER FOUR

Speaking the International Language of Art

I. Who Will Teach the Teachers?

Teaching on U.S. army
bases didn't appeal to many of the American teachers in Europe. Like many of their students, they were homesick. But teaching students and teaching teachers appealed to McGrath precisely because it took him away from home and away from the familiar. Then, too, he felt that he had as much if not more freedom to teach in the military schools as he had in Richland. There was a kind of democracy in the classrooms that he enjoyed; the students came from all over the U.S., and they were white, black, and Hispanic. There was no segregation in the army schools as there still was in much of the U.S., and so for the first time he had students from African-American families. Moreover, in the midst of the Cold War, McGrath brought together Europeans and Americans and reached out to teachers and writers in Eastern Europe and the Soviet Union.

"Sometimes it's better to be David than Goliath,"

he said. "My approach was always to operate under the behemoth. and I found that my best supporters were the parents. They were almost all in the military, but they saw that their kids were getting a good education and that they were also very happy to be in school."

He added, "It was a scary time, a time of darkness in many ways. There was the legacy of the Holocaust and threats to drop atomic bombs. School was one of the few places where young people felt safe and protected."

McGrath went on the road almost continuously during the four years that he held his job as the arts and crafts specialist in Europe, piling up thousands of kilometers. He never reached Ethiopia—one of the countries under his jurisdiction—but he crossed the continent, traveled over the back roads of France, Germany, and Italy, even made it all the way to Sardinia.

48 As he quickly discovered, Europe wasn't as vast as the Pacific Northwest. He could easily drive from headquarters in Karlsruhe, Germany, to Paris in a few hours and then to Orléans in less than a day—in an era before super highways. On the road in Europe, as in the Pacific Northwest, he saw powerful currents of creativity and powerful currents of destruction. World War II was still a raw memory for adults, and European cities still had bombed-out buildings. Even for school children who had not directly experienced it, the war was a palpable presence.

By the mid-1950s, the awful reality of the Holocaust had sunk into the consciousness of Europeans and Americans. Art, literature, and music brought the horrors of World War II into the open. *The Diary of Anne Frank* made a powerful impact on McGrath, as it did on almost all of his contemporaries. McGrath saw the play when it was produced on stage in Frankfurt in 1957;

when it was over the audience sat in stunned silence, too shocked to applaud.

There were other stark reminders of the Nazi past. One of the schools he visited as a teacher of art teachers was at Dachau, the site of the German concentration camp. American teachers were taken on a tour of the facility, and so they learned that the environment around the school was not nurturing. But even an environment that throbbed with human pain and suffering could be educational.

"I remember the barbed wire fence that kept the prisoners inside," McGrath said. "I remember the barracks with the stacks of bunk beds, the room where the Jews were gassed, and then the ovens and the mounds of ashes. It was terribly, terribly, terribly depressing, but it was real and it wasn't simply numbing. It touched a nerve that gave rise to creativity."

In the summer of 1958, when he met Rauschenberg and Johns in New York, he also visited the Museum of Modern Art (MOMA); of all the paintings he saw, the most unsettling and yet the most inspiring was Picasso's *Guernica*; eleven feet tall and 25.6 feet wide, it cried out against the 1936 German aerial bombing of Guernica, the Basque town. It proved to be the opening act of aggression in World War II, and soon the name Guernica echoed around the world.

After gazing at Picasso's painting at the MOMA, McGrath felt he had to see the town that had inspired the artist and, after his return to Europe, he found its stonewalls depressing and the echoes of the Spanish Civil War still daunting after two decades. Then, at Altamira and Lascaux, he saw 30,000-year-old cave paintings which reminded him that art could and would survive anything and everything, even holocausts and madmen like Hitler.

"I went to Lascaux cave with the principal from the American school at Périgueux," he remembered. "I had to lie on my back to see the animals painted with red and black pigments on the ceiling."

He added, "At Lascaux, the colors were principally black and red, but there were also amazing yellows and oranges. I loved the cave paintings; the images of animals—deer, bulls, and aurochs—were phenomenal. They connected with the petroglyphs of the Pacific Northwest, and I recognized once again the energy of art. I have always believed that those cave paintings were for the whole tribe, for everyone, in that long-ago society and not just for the artists who made them."

McGrath gave workshops to foster creativity to classroom teachers in Poitiers, Bussac, and Captieux in France and in Wuertzburg, Heidelberg, and Berlin in Germany. At the American High School in Paris, he held an arts festival; at the American High School in Livorno, Italy, he gave a writing workshop and invited students to describe the port, the fishermen, the boats, and nets. "We're not in America anymore," he told students. "Look at the world all around you."

II. The Big Book of Art

There were hundreds of teachers in the art programs that he designed, and, while he met with a great many of them, he couldn't meet all of them. Years later, when he looked back at his experiences in Europe, he would say, "I should have written a text," and added, "but I had too much else going on." In fact, he did write a book—with help from friends and colleagues—entitled

Arts and Crafts Education for Elementary School Teachers which played a major role in the way that art was taught in the U.S. Army schools. Two hundred mimeographed pages, stapled together, and profusely illustrated, it didn't look like a traditional text, but it offered details about how to teach nearly every art subject, such as puppets, murals, collage, and painting. Each of the sections in the manual he produced—on posters, prints, murals, mobiles, and more—provided a history of the medium and biographical information about the leading artists in the field, such as Toulouse-Lautrec, Albrecht Dürer, Johann Gutenberg, and Diego Rivera.

He urged experimentation, exploration, and hands-on experience, especially with clay, a medium that could be pounded, pressed, rolled, punched, squeezed, cut, folded, ripped apart, and put together again.

Official U.S. Army policy set forth the precise number of minutes per week that art was to be taught in schools. Grades one and two were to have art three times a week and for no more than thirty minutes. McGrath recommended that more time be given to creative expression than the official guidelines allocated, and he found ways to expand the time devoted to art by linking it to traditional academic subjects such as math and science.

When he met with teachers, he urged them to connect art to everything else in the school. He suggested that teachers assign E. B. White's classic for children, *Charlotte's Web*, for example, and make mobiles inspired by the characters in the book.

In a 1958 essay entitled "Making the Most of Materials at Hand," McGrath urged teachers to use materials creatively and to play with them. The concept of "we" should be added to the concept of "me," he insisted. In kindergarten, he suggested that students learn the basics of color, line, and shape, and that, as they became more observant of the world outside themselves, they could move on to portray the individual characteristics of plants, animals, and human beings.

III. Do Not Give the Child the Answer

In his text for art teachers, he devoted a section to the difficult child. For McGrath, the bottom line was, "Do not give the child the answer to his problems; help him find it through careful questioning." He also urged teachers to evaluate student artwork, keep charts, and record the progress of each individual student.

His teaching was child-centered, but he didn't allow the child to dictate the curriculum. Before students began to create art, they had to engage with the world, he insisted. The teacher could provide a bedrock of experience for children by taking the class on a walk, a field trip, show a film, tell a story, enact a skit, and ask questions: How? Where? What? Why?

"Today, so much of the human touch is missing," McGrath said. "Much of the richness is gone, too. In Europe, at that time, we looked at art as human expression. We encouraged all of the arts, and we always fought for art education. Today, in schools where there is emphasis on computer education, students often don't have the opportunity to use their hands when making art. They miss the touch of clay and the sight, right before their own eyes, of real colors running together in a painting. In my gloomiest moods, I think that education through the arts is vanishing and that human beings will become insensitive."

IV. The Opportunity for Creation

All over Europe, McGrath regularly attended music, opera, and food festivals, and he hit upon the idea of bringing festivals into the U.S. Army American schools themselves where he could create an atmosphere of festivity in classrooms and hallways. Children's art was as worthy of celebration, he insisted, as Mozart's symphonies and Wagner's operas, and festivals in schools would, he argued, bring together parents, children, and teachers. Moreover, the U.S. Army—its officers and enlisted men—would see that money spent on art was worthwhile. McGrath edited and published two booklets that were distributed at the festivals he launched, one in Munich in 1961 and another in Frankfurt in 1962.

Both booklets are stamped with McGrath's own unique way of looking at the world. If his Richland students could have seen them, they would surely have recognized the hand of their former teacher. The booklet for the Munich fine arts festival, for example, includes photos that highlight the role of young women and African Americans. McGrath wanted everyone to be acknowledged, especially those individuals marginalized by the culture-at-large.

53

Violet Hunter, a young bright African American woman and an editor of the yearbook for all of the American schools, came to Europe with her family after attending segregated schools in Missouri.

"My father decided that it would be better for his children to be in a military-sponsored, desegregated school in Germany than in a public segregated school in the U.S." she remembered. "It was a good choice, and I was fortunate to have McGrath as a teacher. Skin color didn't matter to him, and it certainly made no difference to me that he was white. In his classroom, he encouraged creativity from everyone, no matter what a student's background or ethnicity. We all learned to make collages, do watercolors, and pen and ink drawings."

McGrath's fine arts booklet integrated images of black students and white students. Nearly everything that could be integrated was integrated. Karen Schlesinger, another of his students, noticed his habit of bringing things and people together. "He wove together everything and everyone into the curriculum," she remembered. "There were no barriers between him and other people."

The drawings and the essays of teachers, parents, administrators, and students co-mingled. McGrath arranged original poems by students alongside poems by the masters of modern poetry such as Rilke and Carl Sandburg, and they in turn nestled next to quotations from Leo Tolstoy and George Bernard Shaw. "I felt that the students and the teachers had something as important to say as Sandburg and Shaw," McGrath explained. "Sometimes they said the same thing, but in a different voice and in a more contemporary way."

A quotation from Albert Einstein provides one of the leitmotifs for one booklet: "The most beautiful thing we can experience is the mysterious. It is the source of all art and science." Viktor Lowenfeld, a leading art educator, provided a short excerpt from his book *Creative and Mental Growth* (1947) in which he emphasizes the "ability to identify with the needs of others"—another leitmotif for the booklet.

McGrath wrote two provocative essays for the fine arts booklet—"Toward Discovery" and "Toward an Answer: Time and Effort." In the first, he noted that in young people creativity was "natural" and "in the majority of adults almost nonexistent." He meant the essays to prompt controversy, he explained, because "it is often the controversial or unique concept that ... places new light within us as creative beings."

In the booklet that accompanied the science fair, McGrath calls for "true observing" which he defines as "going beyond the edges of the tree, into the pitch, the bird nests, the new spring shoots, the sun crawling into leaves in the morning and leaving shadows in the afternoon." He couldn't help but be poetic, and he couldn't *not* ask for "everyday life" to be a "science fair" where individuals would enjoy "the hullabaloo of living higher than a kite."

Perhaps more explicitly than ever before, he commented on the contrapuntal forces contending for the soul of humanity. As the 1950s turned into the 1960s, he recognized the big picture more clearly than ever before. On the one hand, he saw "the rockets, bombs, and destructive forces," and, on the other hand, he saw "the constructive forces" in health, medicine, and scientific exploration. He called for "world communication" so that humanity might be saved, and he asked each and everyone to emerge from "ignorance, lethargy, selfishness, and destruction." Messianic, crusading, and apostolic — he sounded like a man on a mission.

Mary Lou Denning, one of his closest friends and colleagues, called for "team teaching" because it allowed for the flowering of "enthusiasm and desire." Yvonne Schack, another close friend and an elementary school teacher in Munich, emphasized the importance of curiosity. Going to a window in the classroom during a storm and peering outside at the falling snow was an adventure, she explained. It might lead to further explorations and discoveries.

With an eye on the thaw in the Cold War, McGrath included a letter from a Soviet citizen, living in Siberia, who wanted peace. Ray Bradbury, the American science fiction writer, contributed a poem entitled "Harvest" in which he described the enjoyment of his own "private weather."

V. Art Is Emancipator to Man

It was 1960. The 1950s were beginning to recede in memory. Eisenhower and Nixon were no longer in Washington, D.C., John F. Kennedy was president, and there were new possibilities for art, artists, teachers, and students. McGrath was ready to leave Europe and return to the United States. But he had last-minute business to finish, and that business was his own art. During December 1961 and January 1962, McGrath exhibited his work at the Galerie Dorothea Loehr in Frankfurt. The statement he wrote for the exhibit reflects his state of mind as he looked back at his years in Europe and as he prepared to return to the States. He could say truthfully that he'd had a "peak" experience in Europe—a "*gipfelpunkt*," to borrow the German phrase he came to appreciate. "Everything is possible," he wrote. "Art is emancipator to man."

Everyone might have peak experiences, he proclaimed, and everyone might also "discover universality where there are no frontiers." He seemed to be inspired and to be basking in the "hullabaloo" of life itself. Writing of himself in the third person, he said, "McGrath being a teacher knows it is possible to happen to anyone who will take time to open to the things of the earth and sky and stones and crawling things."

56

As though straddling the Atlantic Ocean and looking at both Europe and America, he noted that European art had a longer tradition than American art. He also felt that American art had a sense of innocence and naiveté that Europeans might emulate. Meanwhile, America was quickly developing roots of its own, he observed, though he also warned of the dangers that lay ahead for American painting.

"Art can become narrow like a supermarket," he wrote. "Or as a child becomes narrow if it stays in its playpen too long."

CHAPTER FIVE

Birth Pains: The Institute of American Indian Arts

I. Indians, JFK, and the Sixties

For eleven years, from 1962 to 1973, McGrath lived inside—as inside as a white person could live—the New Mexican Indian world. As a teacher and an administrator at the Institute of American Indians Arts (IAIA), he was also in a rare position to shape Indian culture. In the beginning, he was hopeful, optimistic, and prepared to give unstintingly of himself to create a new school for "the least understood and most misunderstood Americans," as President Kennedy called American Indians in the preface to *The American Heritage Book of Indians*, published in 1962, just as McGrath arrived in the United States after teaching in Europe. In his essay, Kennedy gave the nation an ultimatum. The treatment of Indians would have to improve dramatically, Kennedy exclaimed, or the relationship between the two races would be "marked down for all time as a national disgrace." McGrath shared the new president's sense of urgency and made a promise to

himself to do all he could do to end the disgraceful ignorance about Indians and to stop the shameful treatment
they received.

When he arrived in Santa Fe in May 1962, he felt at
home, though he had never before set foot in the Southwest. From the start, he was spellbound by Santa Fe's
history and intrigued by the desert that reminded him
of eastern Washington where he lived and taught in
the early 1950s at Columbia High School. To McGrath,
Santa Fe seemed as old as the Old World he had left
behind. He was just thirty four, a young man in age
and in spirit and with more experience and wisdom
about teaching after seven years in Europe. In Santa
Fe, he sensed that he had gone back in time to a world
that would not vanish in the wake of super highways,
jet planes, shopping centers, and skyscrapers. If only he
could help to keep the old ways alive, he would feel ful-
filled. He was certain that art could help do just that.

In eastern Washington, he had worked with the
Yakima Indians, and now he was eager to be among
Indians again, helping them, he hoped, to become pilgrims to their own horizons. There was no way he could
or would lead Indians into the future. That wasn't his
way. But he felt that he could travel along the way with
them and learn from them. From the start, students and
teachers helped him to become a pilgrim bound for the
unknown.

McGrath sensed the vitality of the past in the
Indian tribes who would not surrender their cultures
and traditions. The land itself spoke to McGrath, and
he responded instinctively. He had come directly from
Europe without making a detour to the Pacific Northwest to visit his mother and father in Tacoma or to see
his daughters in Portland. He was still not emotionally

healed from the wounds of his divorce and from the
breakup of his family. Flying directly to New Mexico
from Germany made the journey all the more dramatic
than it might have been had he stopped along the way.

He was eager to begin his job as assistant art director at the brand new Institute of American Indian Arts
(IAIA). The word "institute" made it sound grandiose; in
fact, it was a high school just for Indians from all over
the country, though it also offered a two-year college program that went largely unattended. According to legend,
but not according to historical fact, President John F.
Kennedy established IAIA with an executive order. For
years, Kennedy's role as founding father was even posted
on the IAIA website, though no such executive order
has ever been found. Myths and legends had a way of
entwining themselves about IAIA.

In the vernacular of the 1960s, IAIA "was a trip" and
a "hip" place to be. A small school off the beaten track,
it was born at the Bureau of Indian Affairs and with
old-fashioned Washington, D.C., paternalism perhaps at
its best. From the beginning, there was an inherent conflict at IAIA, though no one seemed to notice it, and the
school became a destination and attracted the famous,
the infamous, and the seekers after fame and fortune.
Kennedy didn't create it, but political power from the
highest levels of American government came to bear
on IAIA.

From the start, IAIA broke new ground by taking
students from all over the United States, from dozens of
tribes, and encouraging them to communicate and create
with one another. In its first year, Indians descended on
IAIA from sixty-nine tribes and nineteen states including Alaska, California, Florida, New York, New Mexico,
Oklahoma, Utah, and Washington. McGrath was excited

by the diversity and by the emphasis on making and performing art and not on tests and testing. There was an
academic side and an art side to the institution, though
the arts were its driving force. IAIA was the first school
for Indians to place art at the heart of the curriculum.

In the summer of 1962, when McGrath first arrived
at IAIA, there were eighty-one teachers on the faculty;
fifty nine of them were native Americans. McGrath was
one of twenty-two white teachers. George Boyce, the
superintendent, never formally interviewed McGrath
for the position of assistant art director. From the State
of Washington, Chief Wilson Charley had composed a
letter of recommendation for McGrath, and it helped
that an Indian praised him as an art teacher. Sight
unseen, Boyce—who was a New Deal Roosevelt Demo-
crat—hired McGrath to teach a handful of classes:
painting, Indian aesthetics, design, creative writing,
and museum training. While he was well trained aca-
demically, there was no way he could have been well
prepared for the ferment that unfolded at meetings and
in classrooms.

61

At the start of June 1962, only seventy students were
enrolled at IAIA, and the opening of the school—set for
September—was delayed a month. One of McGrath's
first tasks was to travel with Allan Houser—an
Apache painter and sculptor whose father had fought
with Geronimo against the U.S. military—to recruit
students. In an official car that belonged to Bureau of
Indian Affairs, they went to the homes of Apache, Hopi,
and Navajo families, told them about IAIA, and persuaded many of them to enroll. To elders and kids alike
they were a strange pair: two teachers, two artists, one
of them an Indian and the other a white man. Traveling together for weeks, they became friends; Houser

took McGrath to Mescalero Apache ceremonies in New Mexico and introduced him to his own family members, and McGrath shared stories about his Uncle Nap in the State of Washington.

Their efforts paid off and by October 1, 1962, the institute had nearly twice the number of students it had four months earlier. Many of the students had never met Indians from tribes other than their own. Many of them, as McGrath soon learned, were handpicked by their elders to attend IAIA and were entrusted with the future of the tribe. Everyone who applied to IAIA was admitted, even students with poor grades in math or science. If young men and women from a tribe expressed a passion for writing or painting and submitted examples of their work, the school almost always opened its doors to them.

62

"Some students came from tiny villages without electricity," he remembered. "Some had never slept in a bed with sheets before they came to IAIA. Others had had their mouths washed out with soap for speaking in their own languages and not in English."

Of the eighty one IAIA faculty members who taught art, none were recruited from the Santa Fe Indian School (SFIS), a long-standing local institution for the education of Indians. A few students, like Hank Gobin, a Snohomish Indian soon to be one of McGrath's students, made successful transitions from SFIS to IAIA. Moreover, a few instructors from SFIS were hired to teach academic subjects such as English. But no one from SFIS was hired to teach a single art class.

The Pueblo Indians at SFIS took the decision not to hire them in the field of art as a slap in the face. Indeed, IAIA administrators and teachers disliked the kind of two-dimensional art, usually without background or contemporary feeling, that the faculty and the students made at SFIS. Not surprisingly, the SFIS faculty opposed the establishment of IAIA.

"This is an imitation of the white man's culture," Martin Virgil, the chairman of the All Indian Pueblo Council in Santa Fe, said of IAIA. In *Westways*, the magazine of the American Automobile Society, journalist Anne LaRiviere joined the fray, noting that in centuries past the Spanish Catholic priests superimposed "mission altars" on "Pueblo kivas"—an act she described as "the triumph of church over pagan." Placing IAIA in Santa Fe, she added, was no less momentous, though she praised individual Indian artists who taught at IAIA—including McGrath's colleagues, Charles Loloma and Fritz Scholder, who became a kind of poster boy for American Indian art in the 1960s.

63

James lived on campus in a two-bedroom adobe house. There was a kitchen, a living room/dining room with a fireplace, and a small room where he painted and hung his own work on the walls. He also exhibited his art on campus along with other faculty members who came from all over the United States, all of them aware of the rare opportunity they held in their own hands.

In the early days, he felt that the school was a family without secrets, a family that shared and cared for one another. Sometimes, in the middle of the night, there would be a knock on his door. A student would want to talk about home, homesickness, or an idea for a painting. McGrath sat, listened, tried to help, and realized that sometimes listening was the only help he could give. He liked the fact that everyone ate together, that each teacher was personally responsible for ten students, and that nearly the whole school observed Pueblo Indian dancing on nearby reservations.

In some IAIA classes, students learned in traditional Indian ways by telling stories about the stars, animals, and plants. In other classes, they learned in Anglo fashion by reading textbooks. All students studied Indian and U.S. history; they learned about George Washington and Geronimo. They also took required art courses: Indian aesthetics and an "arts orientation" class. In painting classes, instructors shared the concepts behind Indian art and introduced students to oil painting and watercolor. Every spring the school held Indian food days when classes were cancelled and students prepared and ate whale blubber, salmon, venison, and Eskimo ice cream: lard with blueberries.

Decades later the institute would look back and celebrate the ferment and the creativity of its early years in a program entitled "IAIA rocks the '60s." The high school for Indians sent out vibrations that shook the era, and the era in turn shook the school. But at the time, the shaking often felt more painful than playful; lives were disrupted, new Indian identities were forged, and Indian Power rose out of the New Mexican desert.

McGrath worked closely with Dr. Boyce and, while they were always civil to one another, they were also philosophically and pedagogically at odds with one another. Soon after he arrived at IAIA, McGrath drew up a list of the differences, as he saw them, between "Anglo art" and "Indian art." It didn't take a genius to see that he preferred the Indian way of making art to the Anglo way.

Under "Anglo" McGrath wrote:

> *Art is separate from life.*
> *Art is for the self, the individual.*
> *Art separate from community.*
> *Fame, glory, recognition are the primary ends.*

> *Commercialism and competition dominate.*
> *Ownership is essential.*

Under "Indian" he wrote:

> *Art part of life.*
> *Individual is part of community and nature.*
> *Spiritual development is primary.*
> *Spiritual and material are as one, and brought*
> *together.*
> *Life is process orientated.*
> *Created objects anonymous.*

McGrath wanted the IAIA to "recognize the culture and traditions from which Indians have come." He wanted the school to help make Native Americans "self-aware, self-confident, and self-determining." But he wasn't the superintendent or the art director at the IAIA. He was the third in command, and he was soon caught up in conflicts that expressed themselves across the curriculum and at every level of school life.

65

One of the main reasons for the very existence of the IAIA—as expressed in the school's "Basic Statement of Purpose"—was to persuade Indians to stay in school and prepare them for academic success. McGrath agreed wholeheartedly, but he also bristled when Boyce talked about "salvaging" Indians; to him, the word "salvage" implied that students were junk or waste and not beautiful just as they were.

Moreover, McGrath felt that if Indian students didn't graduate, didn't feel comfortable in school, and even resented the idea of going to school, it was in part the fault of the school. Schools, he pointed out, didn't talk Indian talk and unfortunately didn't see the world through Indian eyes. In fact, in many ways, as he soon discovered, Indian students felt that schools were enemy territory. Moreover, they were wary of school officials who felt that they had to be rescued from their own Indian identities and taught to be white men who could play golf, a game Dr. Boyce insisted, much to McGrath's embarrassment, that Indians had best learn to play.

When McGrath read a poem that a White Mountain Indian girl named Marylita Altaha wrote about school, he shared it as widely as he could and pointed to it as evidence of the harm that schools inflicted on Indians, sometimes knowingly, sometimes not. That Marylita was only nine made her sentiments all the more powerful to him:

> *Have you ever hurt about school?*
> *I have because I have learned*
> *Lots of words from school*
> *And they are not my words.*

McGrath wrote and disseminated a long list of the words that Indians learned in schools that were not part of their traditional cultures and that "hurt" them just as words had hurt Marylita. His list went on for two-pages and included "success," "failure," "expense account," "work week," "compute," "payroll," "bonus," "damnation," "salvation," "Jesus Christ," "fence," "acre," "progress report," "suburban," "lease," "bankrupt," "draft," "stock market," "neurotic," "anthropologist," "computer," "subsidy," "assassin," "real estate," "public domain," and "art."

It became his calling to change the very ways that Indians learned at school and the ways that schools treated Indians, too. Accordingly, he argued that teachers should not impose values from outside Indian culture onto their students, but rather give them the physical and emotional space so that they could express what was inside.

"The big thing was not to give them examples of writing by published authors, but to motivate them to

venture into their own styles of expression," he said. "I
gave them a variety of themes to write about: ancestors,
home life, inner life, and observations about members of
their family. The students were all outstanding; the men
wrote as well as the women, and the Navajo, the Nez
Percé, and the Tlingets were all equally good. They all
had their own unique voices."

At the IAIA, officials from the Department of
the Interior, the Bureau of Indian Affairs, and the
Roosevelt-era Indian Arts and Crafts Board (IACB)
emphasized glory, competition, and rewards for student
work. The rewards went to the heart of the differences
between the Anglo way and the Indian way. In Anglo
society, "fame, glory, and recognition" were primary
ends. "Commercialism and competition dominated." In
the Indian world, "spiritual development was primary."

67

McGrath preferred the Indian way to the white way,
but he was also conflicted. "I questioned the insistence
on competition and prizes, though I usually went along
with them," he remembered. "I thought that competition
and prizes might hinder the creative growth of the students. A young Indian might make a painting of a tee-
pee, sell it, and then be asked to paint ten more pictures
identical to it. That sort of commercialization did occur.
I didn't want to see the mass production of art, though
I also knew that the commercial world didn't always
inhibit and distort creativity. I recognized that Indian
students at the IAIA, like the best students at Columbia
High School, were talented enough and savvy enough to
handle glory and success."

In 1962, the IACB, which was founded in the 1930s,
was alive and well and meddling in the affairs of the
IAIA, though the original board members had long since
died and had been replaced. The new members included

Royal Hassrick, a prolific author of books about cowboys, Indians, and the American West, and Alvin Josephy Jr., a historian who wrote about Indians and who opposed President Eisenhower's policy in the 1950s of terminating much of the autonomy of Indian reservations.

The best-known member of the IACB was the Hollywood actor, Vincent Price, who often visited the school, met with McGrath, and tried to influence the writing students did. Price also aimed to perpetuate his own name by establishing poetry awards for the IAIA students. "He very much wanted competition," McGrath remembered. "He had his own criteria and his own standards. Students submitted their work to him, and he selected the winners. The students won prizes and divided up $200, which was a lot of money, and more than most of them had ever seen."

68

With so many non-teachers such as Price involved in school activities and with so many U.S. government agencies and boards—from the BIA to the IACB—hovering above it and around it, it's remarkable that the IAIA managed to stake out its own unique identity and get off the ground when it did.

"It was a time of real birth pains," McGrath remembered. "But it was a labor of love. I felt that something new and wonderful would emerge so I stuck with it even when I didn't see eye-to-eye with Dr. Boyce."

II. Scholder, the Udalls, and LBJ

Two Indian artists and teachers at the IAIA—Fritz Scholder and R. C. Gorman—helped to invigorate the school and to prevent it from becoming an outpost of the BIA. They also stirred up McGrath's ideas about Indian art and challenged some of the basic assumptions he'd carried around with him ever since his boyhood days with his Uncle Nap.

Born in 1937 in Minnesota, Scholder studied with Wayne Thiebaud in California and joined the Rockefeller-sponsored Indian Art Project at the University of Arizona in 1961 before moving to Santa Fe. McGrath watched as his artistic career evolved and came to admire him for his defiance and directness. Scholder and his art were, as McGrath pointed out, an affront to the American tourists who flocked to the Southwest and who expected Indians to smile for their cameras and behave in accord with white stereotypes of Indians. Part warrior and part magician, Scholder aimed to create order out of the chaos he saw around him. "I attack the canvas," he explained to McGrath. "I paint almost in a trance."

Like many of the other young Indian artists at IAIA, Scholder aimed to explode icons of Indians, and, not surprisingly, his paintings of Indians wrapped in American flags provoked strong reactions from Indians as well as whites. Art critics praised Scholder as a patriotic American and missed the point, he insisted. He did not include the flag in his art to show that the American Indian was a patriotic citizen or because he wanted to depict Indians as genuinely American as everyone else under the same Stars and Stripes. He was merely reflecting reality and recording history. "In the late 1800s, surplus stocks of American flags were sent to the different reservations," Scholder explained to one and all. "These were given out to the Indians who immediately incorporated them in their costuming and became a part of their dress."

In the 1960s, Scholder and his contemporary, R. C. Gorman—who was born in 1931 on a Navajo reservation in Arizona—argued that "Indian" was not a single, fixed identity, but something in flux, and that it was time for Indians to recreate and reinvent themselves. As a young man, Gorman played with many of the stereotypes before he deconstructed them. In 1961, he worked at Disneyland, dressed as an Indian, paddling a canoe, and only later did he carve out his own identity as an iconoclastic artist.

Scholder noted that his own work and that of Gorman helped "Indian artists get out of the clichés they were in." He added, "The world has been shocked back into more of an understanding of what the American Indian is all about. He's not a noble savage. He's real."

No fan of the BIA or the Department of the Interior, Scholder went his own way. About his own creations, he said, "They're not Indian art. They happen to be paintings of Indians done by someone who is of Indian descent." He added, "I have always been an individualist." On the subject of the IAIA, he explained, "It was kind of a merging of contemporary with traditional." There were three distinct elements at the school, he observed: a "high aesthetic sensitivity among the students," a very high "mystical development," and a belief that the land was not private property to be bought and sold. Of course, Scholder's view of the mystical, aesthetic IAIA students was not in accord with George Boyce's view of the golf-playing Indian students pursuing professional careers.

Scholder and Lloyd New—the art director and McGrath's immediate supervisor—held sway at the IAIA and seemed all-powerful to the students. New was known as "the icon" because of his own fierce sense of Indian identity, but the school was under the purview of a white man, Stewart Udall, Kennedy's secretary of the interior, who aimed to merge the interests of the American government and the New Frontier of the Kennedy administration with the genuine needs and the wants of the Indian community. Born and raised in Arizona, a graduate of the University of Arizona law school, and a congressman from Arizona from 1955 to 1961, Udall grew up around Indians and, like Kennedy, wanted to do something to make a difference for them. From Scholder's point of view, the IAIA was "a pet of Udall's"—as polite a slap in the face as he could make without sounding rude or crude. Scholder meant to subvert Udall's and Boyce's "pet" project and make it into a school that would accurately reflect Indian art and culture.

Stewart Udall and his wife, Lee, visited the school and became friendlier with McGrath than with Lloyd New, George Boyce, or anyone else on the faculty, which proved to be a double-edged sword. McGrath's friendship with Stewart and Lee helped to make the IAIA more visible in Washington, and yet it also cut him off from the students and from his administrative supervisors. The Udalls invited him to their home in Virginia and introduced him to writers such as the American poet, Robert Frost, and the British poet and critic, Stephen Spender. Moreover, with Lee Udall, McGrath went to the White House in tuxedo to hear, for example, Pablo Casals, the renowned cellist. He enjoyed the music more than anything else,

Moreover, he attended state dinners in the rarefied company of President and Lady Bird Johnson. For years, he went back and forth from Santa Fe to Washington, D.C., learning to cope with government officials and bringing Indian artists to the attention of the nation and the world. Reporters turned to McGrath when they

wanted news and information about the IAIA, and so
for years he became the institution's necessary, visible
figurehead, and yet his visibility, especially in the media
and at the White House, estranged him from Lloyd New
and George Boyce. Eager to lead students from their
own obscurity into a visible world and yet at the same
time cautious about pushing himself into the spotlight,
James existed in a limbo world in which he was neither
famous nor invisible—a strong presence and yet a presence only on the sidelines. The students, however, were
the best advertisements for the school.

"We really had a sheltered world there," one student
wrote to McGrath after she graduated. "This outside
place is really outside, and a person could go mad very
easily." Still, the school provided students with resources
for survival. "I find a poem. I write a line. I sit and sing
and I am happy," another student wrote McGrath. Yet
another explained that her fellow students at the San
Francisco Art Institute—which Hudson, Wiley, and
Allan attended after high school—were surprised to
learn that she was an Indian. She didn't fit their preconceptions, but that didn't unnerve her. She had
learned at IAIA to have "self-confidence and a sense
of self-dignity."

Indians who graduated from the IAIA remembered
McGrath as a teacher and as a mentor. "It made no
difference to me that Jim wasn't an Indian," Veronica
Orr, a Colville Indian from Omak, Washington, said.
"The soul of a person doesn't know white or red, male or
female, time and distance. I first met Jim when I was
seventeen. At the IAIA, he taught us tribal dances and
invited us to his home where we told one another stories
and learned through friendship."

Kevin Red Star, from Montana, explained, "I was a

Crow Indian, but I hadn't thought about it much until I met McGrath, and he encouraged me to go to the library, read about the Crow, use traditional Crow images, and incorporate aspects of old pottery designs in my art."

Alfred Clah, a Navajo born in 1945, came to the IAIA in 1963 and praised McGrath. "He was still young when I met him," Clah remembered. "He had been in Europe, and he knew a lot of other cultures. He told us about Michelangelo and the Italian Renaissance and opened a world to us." Clah added, "I had been doing realistic painting before I met him; he taught me abstract art, and I have always been grateful to him for that. He also encouraged me to walk around, talk to the wind, the rocks, and the stars. I came to appreciate that art wasn't about making money. Through art you learn not to be afraid of death. When the time comes you have joy in your heart."

James McGrath, three years old, with mother Millie Mae McGrath and uncle Napoleon Bonaparte Bernier ("Nap"), 1931.

Napoleon Bonaparte Bernier.

McGrath with Aunt Sinnie and Uncle Nap, 1948.

*Jim, second row, second from right, dressed up
as an Indian, Edison Elementary School, 1937.*

*McGrath, second from left, after salmon fishing
in Washington, sometime in the 1940s.*

Photo portrait of Jean McGrath, James's wife,
and their two daughters, Jeni and Jain.

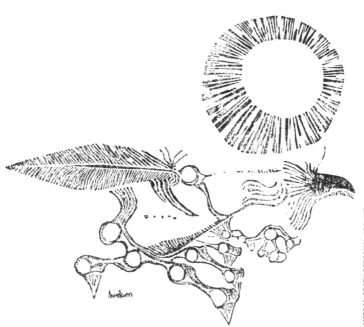

James McGrath, 23, at bulletin board, Columbia High School, Richland, Washington, 1952. Also pictured are students Dorothy Dowis, Diane Dudley, and Richard Roach.

Bob Hudson's untitled illustration from the 1956 Columbia High School yearbook.

Detail from "Grand Coulee Dam," palette knife painting by Bill Allan for the yearbook at Columbia High School, 1954.

JAMES McGRATH PERSONAL ARCHIVE

"Keel boats Along the Columbia," a pen-and-ink drawing by Bill Wiley for the Columbia High School yearbook, 1954.

JAMES McGRATH PERSONAL ARCHIVE

Bill Wiley cartoon from 1955 yearbook.

jim scoggin

✗ My rock is a rough and rugged individual. Its had a hard time all its life. Its been bumped and thumped and crashed and gnashed and blown and torn and pounded and rounded and yet it has survived. It has some penetrations and its busy with partial penetrations. One side is very rough where sand and things have blasted it and the other side, the side it sat on most of the time, is smoother. The rock has little blue or steel-grey areas that make it look like its still cold from the ice age.

My rock is very wise. I suppose all rocks a wise to a certain degree but mine has a high I.Q. to start with. It has given with time. It has absorbed the shocks of life and consequently it is still a whole rock. Maybe it has been worn down a little but it hasn't been broken like many rocks are. Except for one side. On this side a little piece of my rock chipped off. It would have taken many centuries for that piece to rub and wear off but it has been chipped off instead. The whole rock seems sad because of it. I seem to feel that the rock doesn't yet trust me either because of it. Being such a rugged rock it isn't very trusting. I couldn't build up its faith in a day if I had to. It will take much longer. It will take much friendliness on my part. I will have to do all the giving for a long long time before I'll do any receiving. That's good. I should have to earn the benefits of my rock as with all things you should have to earn their benefits

✗ I believe my rock is an introvert. It stays back in its shell and only sees the day through its millions of penetrations. It isn't in the least imposing. It is however very fascinating. It could with time grow into my friend. I'm trying but I'll need some co-operation on its part.

It would be very interesting to be an ant and come upon my rock. There would be so much to do and explore. So many mountains to climb and valleys to look into and caves to search through. A lifetime could be spent finding new things everyday. Never could you know every nook and crany, every canyon and ravine. Yes my rock seems to be a small world in its self. Almost a universe, in its self.

To tell how I feel about my rock would take at least a year and a day. A year to learn to know it in and a day to write in which to tell about it. The longer the better. As I have said my rock isn't ready to be friendly yet

I'm not finished !!!!!

Essay by Columbia High School student Jim Scoggin for assignment by McGrath to find and write about a stone.

Bob Hudson untitled art from 1956 yearbook.

EDUCATION OF DEPENDENTS PROGRAM, U.S. ARMY E
HIGH SCHOOL FEEDER PLAN, SY 1960-61

USAREUR MEMO 621-320-14

LAON

VERDUN

EVREUX

PARIS

CHAMBLEY
ETAIN

METZ

ORLY

VITRY
VASSINCOURT

TOUL

TOUL-
ROSIERES

DREUX

PHALSBOURG

FONTAINEBLEAU

CHAUMONT

VI ORLEANS

LA BAULE

SAUMUR

CHINON

INGRANDES

CHATEAUROUX

POITIERS

CROIX CHAPEAUX

CHIZE
FONTENET

ROCHEFORT

BRACONNE

FRANCE

BUSSAC

CAPTIEUX

PRUE N

SP

B

VERONA

TORINO

VI VI

ITALY

ASMARA

ETHIOPIA

LIVOR

ADDIS ABABA

Map of U.S. Army schools in Europe under McGrath's direction, 1960-1961.

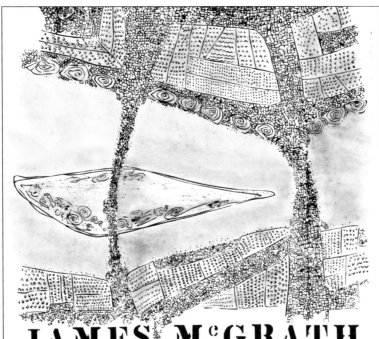

JAMES M^cGRATH

VOM **6 december** verlängert bis 15. januar 1957

ZIMMERGALERIE

FRANCK

FRANKFURT AM MAIN
vilbeler str. 29

Poster for McGrath's art exhibit, Frankfurt, Germany, 1957.

EXHIBITION by the Arts Faculty

INSTITUTE OF AMERICAN INDIAN ARTS / Cerrillos Road / Santa Fe / New Mexico

Opening Preview, Sun. Dec. 12, 2 5 P.M. / Gallery Hours 9 12, 1 4 weekdays / Dec. 13 thru Jan. 16 / weekends by appointment

T. D. ALLEN / LOUIS BALLARD
LEO N. BUSHMAN / ALLAN HOUSER
OTELLIE LOLOMA / MICHAEL McCORMICK
JIM McGRATH / ROLLAND R. MEINHOLTZ
LLOYD KIVA NEW / RALPH A. PARDINGTON
NEIL PARSONS / FRITZ SCHOLDER
TERRENCE W. SCHUBERT / SEYMOUR TUBIS
JOSEPHINE WAPP / KAY V. E. WIEST

Poster for faculty art exhibit at Institute of American Indian Arts.
McGrath, last row, second from right.

McGrath and IAIA student Irene Toledo, ca. 1972.

IAIA faculty member Fritz Scholder previews his painting to colleagues McGrath and Otellie Loloma, ca. 1968.

James McGrath installing an IAIA exhibit. ca. 1971.

*McGrath with ambassador Edward M. Korry and wife at an
IAIA traveling exhibit in Santiago, Chile, 1968.*

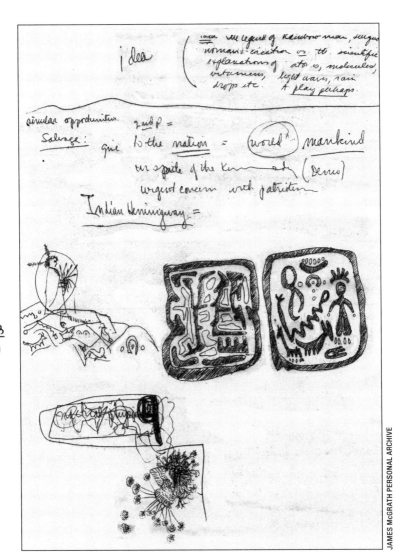

*McGrath's doodles and notes during faculty meeting
at Institute for American Indian Arts, 1962.*

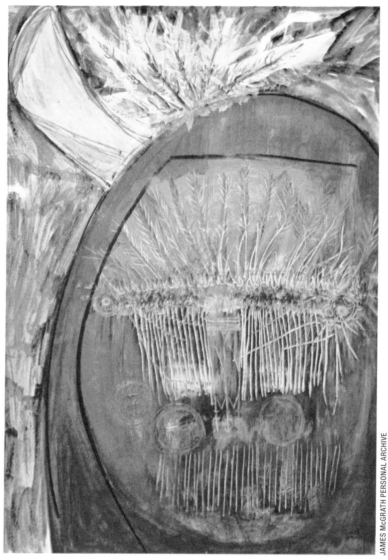

McGrath's portrait of Otellie Loloma, "Sequafnehma," 1964.

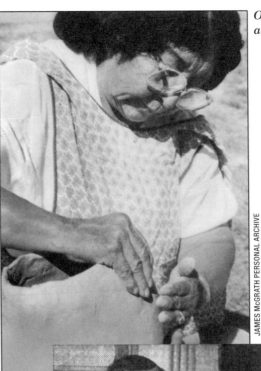

*Otellie Loloma
at work.*

James McGrath and Otellie Loloma in Santa Fe.

FUTURE DIRECTIONS IN NATIVE AMERICAN ART

THE INSTITUTE OF AMERICAN INDIAN ARTS   SANTA FE, NEW MEXICO

Cover for booklet, Future Directions in Native American Art, *designed and edited by McGrath for Institute of American Indian Arts, 1973.*

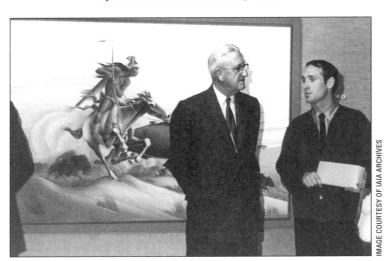

James McGrath with IAIA superintendent George Boyce (painting by Allan Houser in the background), ca. 1965

At a mask-making workshop in Japan for teachers,
U.S. Department of Defense Overseas Schools, 1975.

*McGrath with students and teachers
in Brazzaville, the Republic of the Congo, 1995.*

James McGrath

a retrospective
Markings, Memories, and Mirrors
curated by William Allan

EXHIBITION
May 9 – June 22, 2002
Meridian Gallery
545 Sutter St.
San Francisco, CA 94102
clafouti@earthlink.net
www.meridiangallery.org

POETRY READING
James McGrath , William Witherup,
and Sterling Bunnell
Wednesday May 8th 7:30 PM
Bird & Beckett Books
2788 Diamond St.
San Francisco

OPENING RECEPTION
Thursday May 9th 6:00 - 8:00 PM
Meridian Gallery

ARTIST'S TALK
Saturday May 11th 3:00 PM
Meridian Gallery

*Pamphlet for an exhibit of McGrath's work
at the Meridian Gallery, San Francisco, 2002.*

McGrath with former students Kevin Red Star, Dorothy Dowis, Bill Wiley, Bob Hudson, Bill Allan, Bill Witherup, and Jim Scoggin at the Meridian Gallery.

97

McGrath with students at the Hopi School, Arizona.

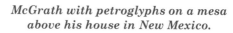

McGrath with petroglyphs on a mesa
above his house in New Mexico.

James McGrath and Jonah Raskin, Santa Fe, 2009.

*McGrath holds an apple from an apple tree
in his own backyard, Cieneguilla, New Mexico, 2010.*

CHAPTER SIX

The White House and Red Power: Art in a Time of Upheaval

I. IAIA: Showcase to the World

100

At the IAIA, McGrath met Lady Bird Johnson, who came to the school as a private citizen curious about the students and their art. She came, too, as the First Lady and as an envoy of the White House to advance the political interest of her husband's administration and the construction of Johnson's "Great Society." Wearing a simple black dress, white pearls, and in her best Texas accent, she praised the IAIA as a model of "free world" education. McGrath met all of the envoys, the emissaries, the artists, and the heads of state. He remembered that José Limón, the Mexican-born modern dancer, came from New York, danced for the students, and then watched them dance Indian dances. He welcomed a troupe of Maori dancers and Léopold Sédar Senghor, the Senegalese poet, president of Senegal, and the renowned creator of the concept of negritude. With the help of a translator—since he spoke French, not English—

Senghor talked shop with McGrath, promising to take back to Africa the lessons he'd learned about maintaining indigenous cultures in the face of assimilation and cultural warfare.

Peggy Guggenheim toured the campus and to McGrath and the students sang the praises of "primitive" art as the most exciting art in the modern world. Beat poet Allen Ginsberg performed work that was peppered with four-letter words, which shocked the older IAIA Indian women who scolded McGrath for inviting such an outlandish person to the campus. But McGrath defended his action. Ginsberg was a contemporary poet, and the Indians ought to know contemporary poetry.

Robert Coates—the avant-garde novelist and art critic who coined the phrase "abstract expressionism" to describe the work of Jackson Pollock and Willem de Kooning—found IAIA bewildering, awe-inspiring, and "enchanting." In an article for the *New Yorker* entitled "Indian Affairs, New Style," Coates wrote that beneath the "conventional appearance" of IAIA, there was "a revolutionary approach to the whole business of introducing the younger generation of American Indians to the intricacies, the complexities, and—above all—the cultural possibilities of modern life."

101

To call it "revolutionary" might have sounded at the time—it might still sound—an exaggeration. But for much of the nineteenth and the early twentieth century, Indians were discouraged from painting because BIA officials didn't regard their expression as art. They were viewed as relics of a way of life that was deemed un-American, un-Christian, savage, and superstitious. Granted, Indians did continue to paint, make art, speak in their own native tongues, but that was often in direct defiance of official U.S. government policy. So it was hardly a distortion to regard IAIA as a revolutionary force. Like most revolutions it created a revolution in the lives of the participants.

In a cover story entitled "Red Power" published in *Life* magazine, Robin Richman wrote that "the IAIA uses Indian culture as a liberating force to draw students out of their apathy and to set them on creative paths." She also noted that in the United States there was a "double rediscovery" of American Indians — by hippies and by Indians themselves. Of the two, "the hippie discovery is most in evidence," Richman concluded.

If the world rushed in to see the IAIA, the IAIA students also ventured into the big, wide world. McGrath traveled almost everywhere that the students and their art traveled. He became an ambassador for Indian art and culture and an impresario for Indian performers and artists. Throughout the 1960s, no one was more responsible for the IAIA's national and international presence than McGrath, though he didn't do it alone. He and the school had the support of Stewart and Lee Udall. Moreover, the Johnson administration made all sorts of resources available to the IAIA: airplanes, hotel accommodations, taxis, and buses.

II. Primitive and Modern

Soon after the IAIA was founded, McGrath brought artwork by the IAIA students to Washington, D.C. The exhibits he installed helped to change the ways that Americans perceived Indians and the ways that Indians perceived themselves. Never before had so many young American Indians had their work displayed in the nation's capitol. Much of it was snapped up by the U.S. government and shipped overseas where it appeared on the walls of embassies in Kenya, Japan, and India.

Lee Udall—one of the school's most eloquent advocates—discovered an unused gallery on the top floor of the Department of the Interior where her husband Stewart held sway. The "lost" gallery, as it came to be known, had been used for decades as a space to store old furniture. Cleaned out, cleaned up, and restored to its original beauty, then given a new name—the Center for the Arts of Indian America (CAIA)—it became a showcase for Indian art. Articles in the press were predictably clichéd and embarrassing for McGrath to read. One columnist wrote, "What the natives of this country have never been able to do by scalping, or by sending chieftains in full-feathered regalia here to plead their cause, and attract attention to their needs, they may now be able to do through their art."

For the first exhibit at CAIA, McGrath's guiding principle was the synchronicity between primitive and modern art. That principle reflected the actual work that students did. Ernest Whitehead, an Apache, depicted traditional Crown Dancers—Apaches wearing large, elaborate "crowns" that towered above their heads. Nathan Jackson, a Tlinget from Alaska, worked in ways that were traditional to his tribe—with totemic figures—though he represented them in new ways—on woodblocks.

Other artists such as Carol Frazier and Alfred Youngman were far more innovative. Youngman worked in mixed media with words as well as images on canvas, and much of his best work, such as "Bird, Rabbit, and Man," was 6 feet x 5 feet and much larger than anything his Apache ancestors would have made.

Frazier, another of McGrath's students, also worked on a large scale. Her "Basket Design" was 6 feet 3 inches x 4 feet 4 inches, and her interpretation of Paiute designs was original, too.

Tradition and innovation were apparent nearly everywhere. A group of Indian musicians formed a band called "the Jaggers" — after Mick Jagger, the lead singer of the Rolling Stones — and played raucous rock 'n' roll with electric guitars and with most of the gestures, clothes, and hair styles of international rock stars. Others continued to beat traditional drums. *Life* magazine's Robin Richland heard both ancient and modern sounds during her visit to the campus. "At the Institute of American Indian Arts, you can even hear the two cultures colliding," she wrote. "Shrill chanting and the beat of tom-toms echo across the campus while the sound of Diana Ross and the Supremes fills the workshops where students are engaged in pottery, sculpture, beadwork, and weaving." McGrath pointed out that the chanting didn't sound shrill to the Indians themselves. Moreover, as he explained to reporters, Indians had borrowed from whites and incorporated aspects of European culture into their own cultures from the beginning of contact with Europeans.

III. Dancing for the President

In 1965, a year after the first IAIA show at the Department of the Interior, McGrath was invited to the White House along with twenty-eight students who were asked to dance traditional Apache and Pueblo dances for President Johnson and his guest of honor, President Maurice Yaméogo of the West African nation of Upper

Volta and other African dignitaries. The dancers, among them Damon Honyaktewa, who was Hopi, and Ramos Suina, who was Cochiti-Pueblo, rehearsed in the East Room where President Lincoln lay in state after his assassination. Emma Plume, a Sioux, was selected to announce the program; McGrath helped her learn and speak French, the language of President Yanéogo, so he'd understand the meaning and significance of the dancers. Their first day in the East Room, the students "whooped and hollered" and were told by the White House staff they were making too much noise. President Johnson was trying to nap. So the rehearsals became quieter.

The chandeliers in the East Room presented a problem; the crowns of the dancers were too high for the Indians to dance without striking and probably breaking the round glass balls that hung from the chandeliers. Either the crown dance would have to be cancelled or the chandeliers would have to be shortened. The White House agreed to remove the lower portions of the glass. The Indians, and McGrath, took that as a positive sign that the White House was willing to make concessions, perhaps merely symbolic, and yet still significant to their sense of personal and tribal identity.

"There was a certain glow that the students had afterwards," McGrath said. "But overall they were unimpressed with Washington, D.C., and with President Johnson, too." After the performance, Johnson shook hands with James, with the students, and with Otellie Loloma, a Hopi artist, and Josephine Wapp, a Comanche, both of whom accompanied the group as chaperones.

There was a state dinner. Neither McGrath nor the Indians had ever seen such a feast: lobster Newberg,

roast sirloin, rissole potatoes with tomatoes and mush-
rooms, salad mimosa, Brie cheese, and a glacé for des-
sert. The *Washington Post* gave the student performers
a rave review. In a news story entitled "Braves Stage
Pow-Wow for VIPs," Maxine Cheshire noted that the
dances were "as exciting as a Technicolor wild 'n' wooly
western." The students tried to break out of stereotypes
and clichés, but the media put them back in the same
old categories and worn-out images.

"Johnson was friendly and folksy," McGrath remembered. "At one point in the evening, he was told there
was a phone call he had to take. It was a crisis. He
got up and left the room. In fact, a bomb had exploded
in the U.S. embassy in Saigon, and though there was
material damage, U.S. Ambassador Alexis Johnson
was uninjured."

Nearly fifty years later, McGrath looked back and
reflected on the relationship between the White House
and the IAIA. "In hindsight, I can see that the government used the Indians," he observed. "Indians and
Indian art were useful tools for the White House. At
the time, however, I didn't see the exploitative aspect.
I was caught up in the details, and I didn't take in
the bigger picture. It also seems fair to say that it was
an exciting time for the Indians from the IAIA, who
received accolades and recognition and who gained self-
confidence. Going to the White House was a real boost
to Red Power, though I'm sure that was not the inten-
tion of the Johnson administration. As the 1960s went
on, it became increasingly apparent to nearly everyone
at the IAIA that the White House tried to use the
Indians to improve its image around the world. Resent-
ments rose quickly and a sense of hurt and anger
became more pronounced at IAIA."

IV. Not a Wild West Show

Indians had been going to Europe to perform for centuries by the time that McGrath and a group of Indian artists went to Edinburgh and then to London and Berlin in 1966 on a four-month tour. Famously, William Cody, aka Buffalo Bill, took Indians to Europe to perform before royalty and heads of state early in the early twentieth century. Buffalo Bill advertised and promoted the staged events as "Wild West Shows," and they were immensely popular, though they hardly presented an accurate view of the American West.

"Our trips to Europe weren't as wild as Buffalo Bill's Wild West shows," McGrath said. "For one thing, there was no shooting, no 'bang bang.' Moreover, what we were doing was not as dishonest as his shows. We were forthcoming about Indian life and traditions. We were true to Navajo culture and true to the whole spirit of the IAIA."

In 1966, his first destination was the Edinburgh Festival where the lord mayor formally greeted them, and Lee Udall met them, along with Yeffe Kimball, a white woman who was passing as an Osage artist and doing a very good job, too. IAIA teachers and students were all fooled.

Eighty percent of the Indian artists in the Edinburgh show were the IAIA students or graduates. European art critics couldn't help but notice that while Europeans were turning to primitive art for inspiration, American Indians were turning to European modernism. After the success of the Edinburgh show, Lee Udall telegraphed McGrath in her inimitable whimsical fashion: "Jim. Stop. We have a program on the moon. Stop. Are you interested? Stop. Lee. Stop."

McGrath didn't have a moment to reply; he was on to the next city and the next exhibit. He was inclined to go everywhere and anywhere, and though he didn't, of course, make it to the moon with Lee, he took the exhibit and the Indians who accompanied it across Europe.

Fred and Bertha Stevens, a Navajo couple, traveled with McGrath. From Santa Fe, they flew to Scotland, then to England and the Horniman Museum in London, where a billboard proclaimed "Red Indian Fred and His Squaw." Next it was on to Amerika Haus in Germany and then to Turkey where they visited Hittite archeological sites and where Bertha Stevens met women weavers and exchanged weaving lore with them. Fred created Navajo sand paintings in Edinburgh and London and donated them to museums, but in Germany he refused requests to leave them behind. Once again McGrath found himself in the thick of controversy.

108

Fred Stevens refused requests to speak his native language, and McGrath sympathized with him when he said, "I am a Navajo, and I will not speak my language to your people here in Germany." Stevens made his remarks to representatives of the U.S. state department and to the curator at the Dahlem Museum in Berlin. World War II and the fight against fascism were still vivid memories for Fred, who served in the U.S. military; he would not let down his guard in Berlin.

The Germans were doubly disappointed; they learned that Fred and Bertha weren't Sioux; to them the Sioux in headdress epitomized the American Indian. At times, it seemed surreal to McGrath. "If someone had told me in 1953 or 1954 that I would be educating Europeans about Native American art, I probably would have laughed at them," he said. "It would have seemed unbelievable, and it certainly was stretching the role of the art teacher further than I would have imagined."

McGrath gave lectures about sand painting, weaving, and Navajo culture. With two durable slide projectors and two separate sets of images, he showed pictures of New Mexican faces and places, talked about Indians and their environments, and informed audiences about Indian creativity. Louis Ballard—IAIA's director of music programs—made top-quality recordings of Indian music that McGrath played, and that helped to create the ambiance for the lectures and slideshows. McGrath also read American Indian stories, myths, and legends that he culled from Margot Astrov's indispensible anthology, *The Winged Serpent: An Anthology of American Indian Prose and Poetry.*

In 1967, the Indians, the exhibit, and McGrath went to Santiago, Chile, where Fred drummed with Mapuche Indian men. Then they were off to Argentina where McGrath's talks about art were translated into Spanish. For much of 1967, he worked around the clock, attending luncheons and dinners sponsored by the U.S. state department, visiting museums and art galleries, and meeting local citizens interested in folk art and the indigenous cultures of the Americas. In 1968, McGrath, Fred, and Bertha went on the road again—this time to Mexico City where artwork by more than a dozen American Indian artists was exhibited. McGrath installed paintings by Bill Prokopiof, an Aleut, Doug Crowder, a Choctaw, and Willard Stone, whose "Cherokee Madonna" attracted large and appreciative crowds. The exhibit also included T. C. Cannon's bold eye-catching oil painting that featured the New Mexican landscape and that he playfully entitled "Mama and

Papa Got the Shiprock Blues." Viewers were tickled by Cannon's work.

But for McGrath, the whole Mexico City jaunt was the least successful and the least satisfying of all the journeys he made for the IAIA. Essential supplies were unavailable, and he had to improvise. One night he and Fred scooped up sand from a Mexico City construction site for Fred's sand paintings. That method was easier than going through red tape. Mexico City reverberated with gunfire the summer of the 1968 Olympics — the summer when the world seemed to teeter on the brink of disaster. In the Tlatelolco section of the Mexican capital, government troops shot and killed protesting students. It was a bloody summer, a bloody year that seemed to get under James' skin and to rankle him. Still, there were satisfying moments even in bloody Mexico City.

"We were given a space in a refurbished nunnery along with arts and crafts exhibitors from other countries," McGrath said. "We opened the eyes of a great many people in Mexico City to native culture in the United States. We also gave South American artists, poets, and playwrights an idea of what they might do in their own countries, which were often unwilling to recognize their own indigenous populations."

In his official report to the U.S. Department of State, McGrath was unenthusiastic about Mexico City. "I do not feel the exhibit was well-used, the potential was not realized, the story of the contemporary United States Indian in the world of art was not really exposed," he wrote. But he didn't quit. He made recommendations for improvements, including a catalog to be printed in Spanish as well as English, and he suggested that a refurbished exhibit head for Peru,

Bolivia, Ecuador, Colombia, and "other countries with Indian populations."

V. Art in an Age of Indian Nationalism

In 1968, McGrath returned to the IAIA, changed by his intense experiences in Europe and South America. The IAIA had changed, too, and he noticed the new gestures, phrases, and attitudes. Students put up posters that proclaimed "Red Power" as well as posters with images of Geronimo, the famed Apache Indian warrior who was born in 1829 and died in 1909. Geronimo became, in the 1960s and 1970s, a hero to Indians and hippies because of his expertise as a warrior and his deep soulfulness.

McGrath wrote and delivered a lecture on the changes at the IAIA. He gave praise, but much of his talk was critical of the institution. Communication was inadequate, he insisted. Cooperation was sorely lacking. Moreover, he criticized teachers who were "rigid, cautious, and conventional." He didn't name names or single out specific teachers for rebuke. Rather he criticized "the system" and the "years of stereotyped training" that instructors received in teacher training programs in colleges.

For the most part, McGrath sided with the students, supported their demands for relevant courses and training, and identified with their cause. "Students have to have a stronger voice," he said. Moreover, he also identified himself with the growing Red Power movement and praised American Indians because they had "taught themselves for thousands of years without books, or school buildings, or course outlines."

111

Increasingly, he was in a difficult if not impossible position. Administrators were supposed to impose rules, raise money for new buildings, and make sure faculty members taught their classes and graded exams. Now, he chafed under the role of administrator. McGrath caught the 1960s bug that spread across the nation and that inoculated teachers and students with the idea that it was essential to revolutionize American education. McGrath called for "sensitive, skilled teachers," urged them to understand their students, and invited them to ask essential questions such as, "Who am I?"

To help answer the question, he offered the words of Marylita Altaha, the nine-year-old White Mountain Apache girl whose poem about hurtful school he could never forget, as well as the words of Dave Martin Nez, a twenty-year-old Navajo, who wrote:

> *We shall learn all the devices of the white man ...*
> *But we'll retain our beauty*
> *And still be Indians.*

In the early 1970s, McGrath wondered about his identity as an Anglo in an Indian world in the throes of a rebirth of nativism, tribalism, and nationalism. "Who am I"? he asked himself. His question didn't stop him, however, from teaching and writing. In many ways, the years from 1970 to 1973 were his most creative and productive at the IAIA. He applied for and received funds from Washington, D.C., under Title One, a federal program intended to improve the quality of education in America.

He used the funds to purchase a van, equip it with art supplies, and send it out with a driver, of course, to remote Indian villages in the Southwest. The money also enabled McGrath to hire a teacher—his longtime colleague, Mary Lou Denning, with whom he shared a great deal pedagogically. Denning went on the road and brought art and art supplies to students and teachers. Everywhere she went in Arizona and New Mexico, she took photographs, gathered Indian poetry, and brought it back to Santa Fe where it was exhibited.

The funds from Washington, D.C., laid the groundwork for the production of four beautiful booklets designed by McGrath and illustrated with photos and drawings. He entitled the first booklet, *Art and Indian Children* (1970). McGrath produced three others: *Dance With Indian Children* (1972); *Future Directions in Native American Art* (1972); and *My Music Reaches the Sky* (1973). He had ample help from four IAIA artists and instructors: the musicologist Louis Ballard; Josephine Wapp, a Comanche who taught traditional dances, weaving, and bead work; and Juan Valenzuela, a choreographer who trained with Martha Graham and taught her style of modern dance.

113

Lloyd New, now the director of the IAIA following George Boyce's retirement, also helped to shape the content and the political drift of the pamphlets. Indeed, the future of the IAIA was made abundantly clear in *Future Directions in Native American Art*. All of the words in the title reflect the changes that were taking place at the school and all across the country where Indians lived and worked. It was the future that mattered now, not the past. Direction was all, not confusion or a sense of aimlessness and purposelessness. "Indians" were "Native Americans," much as "Negroes" were now "African Americans," and "girls" were "women." In *Future Directions in Native American Art*, New wrote that his own people had "suffered hundreds of years of cultural decimation as the result of programs deliberately aimed toward the destruction of their cultural lifeways."

Ten years earlier, that language had been foreign to him. These were different times. Now, he spoke in an overtly political way and as though fueled by deep-seated hurts and anger. Moreover, New explained that in the future "the institute shall he staffed primarily with Indian scholars and cultural leaders from the Indian world." The handwriting was on the wall; it had been building steadily for years. No non-Indian teachers were wanted at the IAIA.

McGrath heard the message and knew that his days at the IAIA were numbered. Perhaps if he had been a lowly instructor, he might have been able to stay and teach. But he was publicly associated with the school and had been for a decade. In Washington, D.C., he was the face of the IAIA and now the IAIA wanted an Indian face in the nation's capital and around the country. It was, however, an uncertain time for the IAIA; what had existed in the past—whether it worked or not—was known and safe; what might be in the future was, like most change, unknown and frightening.

McGrath sensed the anxiety in the Indian world and captured much of it in the last of the booklets he produced. He highlighted a quotation from a talk entitled "The New Exodus" by Vine Deloria Jr., the author of the best-selling book *Custer Died for Your Sins: An Indian Manifesto* (1969), which shook up Anglos and Indians and invited them to rethink ideas about Native Americans. Deloria's quotation expressed the feelings of nearly everyone at the IAIA. "We have left the comfortable land of assimilation and have been thrust into the outer darkness of ethnicity," Deloria declared. "Every tool that we have to gather information to find our way was designed for a world of assimilation and integration."

Now, Indians had to find their own way independent of Anglos much as African Americans felt they had to find their way without the help of whites and as the women's liberation movement insisted it had to make a path without men.

McGrath captured the mood of that heady moment in history in a twenty-five-minute documentary film entitled *Two Indians: Red Reflections on Life* that he co-produced and co-wrote. The Mineola, New York, school district collaborated on the project. As the title indicates, the documentary focuses on two individuals—Mark Romancito, a Zuni from New Mexico; and Richard Ray Whitman, from the Yuchi, a small tribe in Oklahoma—though it also offers a larger Indian perspective on life. A dozen or so Native Americans also appear on screen. "Indians don't need the BIA," one IAIA student says. Another explains, "All the Indian wants is to be an Indian and to decide how much of your culture I want, instead of having it laid on me."

In the movie, McGrath integrates images of traditional and contemporary Indian ways. The camera moves back and forth, for example, from scenes of Indians drumming and chanting to clips of the Jaggers, the Native American rock 'n' roll band. McGrath ended the film with Indians dancing in the darkness illuminated only by a bonfire.

In *Two Indians*, students talk on camera about their parents and grandparents, sometimes favorably, sometimes critically, and about the differences between life on the reservation and life in cities. "It feels good to go home to the village," one student says. "The reservation—that's home. We come back here from inner cities, to places where we were born and raised in traditional ways, where we grew corn and where we can worship our Indian gods."

McGrath began the booklet, *Future Directions in Native American Art*, with a quotation from IAIA student Emerson Blackhorse Mitchell, a Navajo from Shiprock, New Mexico:

> *I stand upon my miracle hill.*
> *The wind whispers in my ear.*
> *I hear the songs of the old ones.*

The songs of "the old ones" are more pronounced in the last booklet than in the first booklet, and "Indianness" and "Indianism" are more pronounced, too. McGrath wrote introductions for the first two booklets, but not for the last two. He took a backseat and allowed Indians to speak for themselves. In *Future Directions in Native American Art*, there is almost nothing by non-Indians, and, though McGrath did as much work on the last booklet as on the first three booklets, he scaled back his visibility. On page 31 of *Future Directions*, he appears in the background of a small black-and-white photo of the faculty. A year later, in 1973, he was no longer even in the background at IAIA or in any photograph of the faculty. The school underwent a revolution, and there was no longer room for him.

"The American Indian Movement (AIM) came into the school with a bang," McGrath remembered. "It woke up a lot of people. After AIM came, some students would not come to my classes, and the staff didn't cooperate. That hurt."

He added, "Almost all the white people were ignored. I felt as if I didn't exist, and yet that experience was also very useful. It made me see and realize on a deep personal level what the Indian students, their parents, great-grandparents, and ancestors had gone through for hundreds of years. They were ignored by white society. They were invisible. I realized how painful it was not to be seen. It was a profound learning experience."

VI. Break-Up and Make-Up

McGrath worked at the IAIA for more than a decade. He made close friendships with Indians, and now those friendships were on the line. He worked closely with Lloyd New, and now they were on opposing sides of a vast cultural divide. "Our relationship changed," McGrath said. "It was less cordial than it had been. Lloyd knew that I was in a predicament. We both knew that something had to give because I was a white person in a time of Red Power."

Then, too, McGrath's relationship with Otellie Loloma, his most intimate friend, was profoundly affected. "I conferred with Otellie," McGrath remembered. "She remained friends with me as did some of the students. I did not ask her or anyone else to side with me. I accepted the situation. Of course, Otellie was also caught up in the situation. We all were."

Little by little, McGrath withdrew from friends and colleagues. He gave up his teaching responsibilities. Then pressure mounted for him to step down as administrator, too. Suddenly, without fanfare or an official farewell, he was not around, his house empty. He accepted a job as art director for the Department of Defense Dependent Schools (DODDS) in Asia that enabled him to make a lateral transfer from the Department of the Interior to the Department of Defense. "I left as soon as I could," he said. "It was essential that I get out fast, and once I had a plane ticket I was gone."

During his next-to-last year at the IAIA, he was enrolled in the M.A. program at the University of New Mexico in Albuquerque where he wrote a research paper on "The Training of Native Americans in Education Through the Arts." He began his paper with a quotation from the autumn 1972 issue of *Akwesasne Notes*, the Indian newspaper published by the Mohawk Nation: "If Indian culture shall be taught to Indian students, then the teaching shall be done by an Indian who practices and lives the said culture."

McGrath agreed. One of the main points of his M.A. thesis was that Indians should teach Indians and that Indians who had "life experiences" and no degrees should be valued by educators as much as Indians with college degrees. Moreover, he suggested that Native American teachers could "best succeed" with their students if they used "traditional Indian teaching methods of storytelling, dance, music, and oral expression in the arts."

Most programs for the training of Indian teachers were, he explained, "negative, patronizing, and lacking dignity and respect." He believed that by learning about Indians, the whole country could discover "something beneficial to all American society." At the end of his M.A. paper, he offered definitions for seven crucial words that he felt all Americans should learn and understand: "Native American," "Indian," "Creativity," "Culture," "Traditional," and "Contemporary." From those seven words, he believed, a whole new world of education might be created.

When he left the IAIA, McGrath wasn't gone forever from the world of the Indians or the IAIA. In

1976, he worked with KAET, the PBS-TV station at Arizona State University in Tempe, to make a series of documentaries about seven American Indian artists, some of whom he knew personally from the IAIA: Allan Houser, Charles Loloma, Fritz Scholder, and R. C. Gorman. The other artists in the TV series were Helen Hardin, Joseph Lonewolf, and Grace Medicine Flower, all of whom he met. Of his friends, only Otellie wasn't a part of the documentary.

Gorman spoke for many of his fellow artists in the series when he observed, "There is no such thing as contemporary Indian painting. There are contemporary Indian painters, but I hope they have no special characteristics to identify them as such." He added, "I think that Indian painting shall have made a contribution to American culture on the day when I can walk into a bookstore and pick up a book titled American Painters and find that Indians are included."

The *American Indian Artists* series, for which McGrath wrote the narrative, was broadcast in 1976, the year of the Bicentennial, and rebroadcast dozens if not hundreds of times afterward on PBS stations around the country. Jamake Highwater criticized the series in an article published by The *New York Times*, entitled "My Reservations About That Indian Series." "What is mostly lacking in 'American Indian Artists' is a sense of history that could place the artists in some kind of context and could provide viewers with a basis for comprehending where their unique art comes from," Highwater wrote.

Granted, the series is short on history, but it does enthusiastically celebrate the diverse arts of Indian America, including artists from IAIA, which, KAET's J. Z. Grover wrote in an article in *Arizona Highways*, had "assembled the largest and most varied Indian arts faculty ever gathered."

The TV series enabled McGrath to re-establish links to the IAIA and to heal the emotional wounds he suffered when he was forced to leave the school in 1973. "Working on that project, I believe that I came as close as an Anglo can come to express an Indian way of being in the world," he remembered. "It helped, of course, that I knew many of the artists and that I saw them at work. I observed Scholder in his study and I visited Gorman, who was a wild man and who always enjoyed a party. I liked the voluptuous women in his paintings. I got to know Helen Hardin, too, in Albuquerque and appreciated the matriarchal influence in her work and the way that she blended the ancient and the modern, for example, in 'Masks After Picasso,' which is a brilliant piece."

120

In 1988-89, McGrath went back for a year as the dean of the IAIA. It was a transitional period; the institute was in the process of emancipating itself from the Bureau of Indian Affairs and becoming autonomous and with a board of directors. Funding would continue to come from the federal government, but from now on there would be private funding, too. The school needed a new direction and new leadership; enrollment was down, morale was at a low point, and relationships between students and teachers had soured. McGrath saw it as his job to repair the damage that had been done and to create healthy connections between faculty and students.

"It was the most difficult job I ever had," he said. "The faculty was entrenched and with attitudes that verged on paranoia. 'Will I lose my job'? they would ask me. 'Do I have to work eight to five'? 'Will I have a cut in pay'? The questions were endless."

McGrath wrote a new mission statement that was adopted by the school, though his name was never attached to it. He lobbied for non-graded classes for students, and he tried to "humanize" what looked to him like "a toxic environment." He also realized that some things were beyond his control. He couldn't heal all of the school's rifts, and in April 1989 he wrote a letter of resignation to William Johnson, the new chairman of the Board of Trustees at the IAIA. "I'm happy to say," he wrote, "that I was a part of the IAIA's survival, continuation, and transformation."

McGrath learned immensely from his IAIA experience, and he was eager to pass it on to others. "I would say this to those who want to teach Indian children and who are not Indian themselves: learn about Indian culture and Native American history," he said. "When you arrive on the job, look and listen, especially to the elders because they will be your teachers. In fact, they will be teaching you more than you will be teaching them. Be involved in the community. Ask questions. Find out what is acceptable behavior. Don't go where you are not invited. Respect and honor the culture of the Indians."

What he learned at the IAIA, he brought with him to his next adventure in teaching. For the rest of his life, he reminded students and teachers that an oral culture existed before the arrival of Columbus in the Americas and that stories about and by Indians came centuries before Longfellow's "Song of Hiawatha."

Oral literature had as much value as written language, McGrath told students. To buttress his argument, he introduced them to Nezahualcoyotl, the fiftteenth-century Aztec poet whose songs were often about healing and had touched his own heart. "Indians lived close to the land, in communion with the land," he explained. "The Indian connection to the earth and the sky is the central principle of their lives."

CHAPTER SEVEN

Asia: On the Cutting Edge of Multicultural Art

I. Tea Time in Japan

From 1973 to 1985, McGrath worked as the arts and humanities coordinator for the American schools in Asia under the jurisdiction of the U.S. Department of Defense. He lived in Japan, thousands of miles from Santa Fe, and from the start he was curious about almost everything he saw and heard in Japan, from billboards and neon signs to TV and music. It was obvious to him that the Japanese had their own culture, and yet they also borrowed many things that were American, from baseball to jazz, which made them all the more intriguing in his eyes.

Of course, McGrath stood out in nearly every crowd. Almost everywhere he went in Japan—aside from tourist haunts in Tokyo and Kyoto—he was the only American. He saw a Japan that tourists rarely if ever saw: the insides of Japanese shrines, bars, movie theaters, and Japanese homes. Japan took him to new horizons.

Though he didn't speak Japanese—languages never

came easily to him—he moved freely about the country—in rural areas and cities—and met Japanese teachers, workers, and farmers. His best friend, Tadao "Rio" Suzuki, a Japanese impresario who brought American artists to Japan, took him under his wing and introduced him to traditional Japanese theatre in which masks played a big part and which McGrath, given his experience with the stage and the art of performance, found fascinating.

To his American ear, Japanese sounded stranger than German, French, and Italian, which he learned in bits and pieces in Europe in the 1950s and 1960s. It seemed far too difficult to master Japanese, and so when he arrived in Japan in 1973, at the age of forty four, he decided to explore the culture nonverbally as much as possible, acquainting himself with the customs of the country. Before he could ask American teachers to embrace Japanese culture, he would have to embrace it himself.

After years of teaching, he knew that he learned best by awakening his own sense of touch, taste, hearing, seeing, and smelling, not by sitting passively in a library, listening to a lecture, or memorizing a text. He had an intuition that American teachers and students would learn as he did by swimming in the crosscurrents of Japanese culture.

He promptly enrolled in classes in traditional Japanese arts: *sogetsu*, Japanese flower arrangement; and *shakuhachi*, Japanese flute. For eight years McGrath also took lessons in the Edo Senkei school of tea ceremony from his landlady, Mrs. Osato, who taught him everything she knew and explained that he could make up some of his own ceremonies. Variations were encouraged, he was happy to learn.

At the end of his course of study, he received a certificate to teach the tea ceremony and came away from the experience feeling that he had glimpsed some of the soul of Japan. "I know that I am part of a larger world now than when I lived within the boundaries of the United States," he observed.

He was the only American—and the only male—in Mrs. Osato's class and had the opportunity to observe and to interact with Japanese women, who seemed on the outside tranquil, peaceful, and reserved and rarely revealed their innermost selves. "I felt I was like them," he said. "I saw myself as a private person and I empathized with the women in Mrs. Osato's tea ceremony class. By empathizing, I was able to learn from them and about them."

Mrs. Osato's first name he never learned; in Japan, he discovered, students rarely if ever called teachers by their first names. Of course, his own students didn't call him by his first name, either. Still, there were differences between pedagogy in the United States and in Japan. In Japanese classrooms, group exercises were often more common and individual work less emphasized than in many classrooms in the U.S. Teachers used blackboards differently, too, McGrath observed, to trace the origin and the evolution of an idea, not to write down a concluding statement to be memorized by pupils.

If McGrath had tried to situate himself in a culture dramatically unlike his own, he probably could not have made a better choice than Japanese. After he left the IAIA, he knew that he couldn't retreat to the confines of the white world or blend into Middle America. He certainly didn't want to go back to Richland or Tacoma. Once again, he chose to be a kind of outsider—a white person in a largely non-white world—or perhaps he might have said that he wanted to be a person who aimed to connect with others, irrespective of race and nationality.

"It seemed more exciting to me to go to Asia than look for a job in the States," he said. "I had long been fascinated with Asian cultures. My aunt, Margaret Norman, took me to see Asian art in Seattle when I was a boy, and I liked the ways that Asian art showed up in the work of Morris Graves and Mark Tobey, those two giants of Pacific Northwest art whom I discovered when I was in college."

McGrath felt comfortable in Asia and comfortable teaching again on American bases, though feeling comfortable wasn't his goal. In fact, discomforts seemed to go hand-in-hand with learning. It helped that he knew teachers and administrators, such as Don Nolder and Harold Price, from his days in Europe. Now they were in Honolulu, Hawaii, keeping an eye on the American schools all over Asia. Moreover, McGrath also knew what to expect from military officers who belonged to a tribe of their own, he would say, not unlike the Sioux, the Navajo, and Hopi, and with rites, rituals, and ceremonies of their own.

126

U.S. bases in Asia were largely devoid of art. One might say they were antithetical to art, but after twenty years of making and teaching art, McGrath knew how to make and teach art in largely artless worlds. Moreover, he knew how to persuade military officers to accept the idea that it was in the national interests of the U.S. for the children of soldiers to draw, paint, fly kites, make paper, learn bonsai, origami, and basket weaving.

"In every subject we taught in the schools in Asia, we always went against specialization," McGrath remembered. "We were deliberately and consciously anti-elitist, too. No art teacher could just do his or her own thing, though some wanted to. We made it clear that they had to branch out, work with others, and teach across the curriculum. Moreover, we always emphasized both the global and the local."

In Europe in the 1950s, he had had no advanced degree, and administrators held it against him that he hadn't completed his M.F.A. at the University of Washington. Now he had an M.A. from the University of New Mexico in Albuquerque, a longer resume, more bargaining chips, and more self-confidence.

McGrath's twelve years in Asia were among the happiest of his life. He had tremendous freedom to develop the curriculum for the arts and the humanities, and he had the sense that in Asia he was on the cutting edge of the multicultural. In Japan, Korea, and the Philippines, American students belonged not to one but to two or three different cultures. Their multicultural experiences would soon become the norm for students all across the U.S.A.

In his own boyhood, a student was "white," "black," "Indian," or "Asian." Now a student was Asian American or African American. That cultural reality demanded more innovative approaches to art education than those of the past, McGrath insisted, if children were to participate in their own learning. All across Asia, young American teachers joined with him to experiment in the brave new world of multicultural education and to forge a family of instructors that transcended national boundaries.

Education in Asia in the 1970s was far more centralized and bureaucratized than it had been in Europe in the 1950s, in part because the U.S. was at war in Vietnam. Everyday, on TV and in newspapers, McGrath saw and read stories about American planes bombing Vietnam. The war was in his face. Sometimes the parent of a student did not return from Vietnam and sometimes a parent became a prisoner of war. To McGrath, the stress in the classroom seemed palpable, especially on U.S. bases—like Clark in the Philippines—where wounded soldiers arrived on the tarmac almost daily, a constant reminder of the not-so-distant battlefield.

Like most innovative teachers, McGrath knew how to play by military rules and how to break the rules, too. "There were rules up the wazoo," he remembered. "The only way to get around them was to be positive, optimistic, and to include everyone, including the military brass. We had glowing articles about our work in *Stars and Stripes*, the military newspaper, and we always acknowledged the contributions of people on the base, from generals to privates." The military provided essential resources and materials so that instructors could teach American children the arts and the humanities, including the arts of peace, too, in a world at war.

128

II. The Keep-Moving Mantra

McGrath made up many of the rules as he went along. "Sometimes I blundered ahead," he remembered. "But I always kept moving—that was my mantra: don't stop moving. Occasionally I used subterfuge, but I always brought in the teachers and included them. I never imposed anything from above. That would have backfired." Still, for all his cooperation, he was the authority and in charge. He was responsible for all the programs in the arts and the humanities in forty schools with 2,500 teachers and 27,000 students.

It was bigger than the job he held in Europe. Asia was, of course, larger than Europe with more languages, cultures, tribes, religions, and different kinds of families and governments. At times, the diversity was mind-boggling, though it was also awe-inspiring, especially when he got out of his office, ventured off the beaten track, and discovered whole worlds: temples, open-air markets, bakeries, shrines, caves, breweries, beaches, mountains, jungles, workshops for artisans, shops for tailors, police stations, zoos, factories, and restaurants serving food he never knew existed when he lived in the U.S.

All of Asia was a living classroom that expanded beyond the known, the predictable, and the ordinary. Nearly every day felt like a commencement, and that provided opportunities to bring students and teachers along on his adventures so that they could look, smell, and touch little worlds and big worlds, too, which sometimes frightened them but which they eventually also explored.

129

"Field trips into the surrounding communities became a way of life," he said. "They were a kind of pedagogy. The students came back to school and wrote mini-books. Teachers went on the field trips, too, and developed new ways of seeing and sharing."

His closest American colleague in Asia was Betty Taira, an enterprising school principal eager to join with him and experiment. An Okinawan-American who was born in California, she was interned, along with thousands of other Japanese Americans, under Executive Order 9066 during World War II. By the time McGrath met her, she had acquired a quiet wisdom born of her own experiences in the U.S. and in Asia.

"People asked me how I could have taught on military bases when American soldiers with rifles came to my family's house and took us away," she said. "I learned from the internment years about injustice based on race, and though it didn't make me bitter, it embittered my parents. I didn't want to become like them. When I became a teacher, I always told teachers and students that it's important to treat all people—no matter what the color of their skin or the shape of their eyes—with respect and dignity."

Taira had a degree from the University of Maryland. She taught in Washington, D.C., then in Hawaii, and kept moving until she became a school principal in Okinawa during the Vietnam War. It was a time she remembers as "terrible, terrible—a time when some of our leaders ran amuck." It was also a time when it seemed imperative to reach students about vital issues that affected their lives. She and James worked together in the classroom and on field trips. They taught students whose fathers were American and their mothers Egyptian, for example, or who had American mothers and British fathers.

130

"That's what happens when American troops are stationed around the world," Taira said. "They marry people from other countries and have children who don't belong to a single culture. We introduced those children to all the arts and cultures of Asia."

The cultures sometimes clashed, and sometimes children were confused, angry, and sad, but schools provided a place to make sense of the conflicts and create individual identities.

McGrath traveled in airplanes, provided by the U.S. Air Force, to Japan, Okinawa, Korea, Taiwan, the Philippines, and to Hawaii, too, where for several summers he coordinated an intensive program for art teachers.

Wherever he traveled, he lived close to the indigenous cultures, eating the food of the locals, learning who was revered by the community—it was often an older man or woman—and where and how people respected the sacred.

III. Not in Kansas Anymore

"I thought that I'd been teaching the multicultural—without using that word—for a long time," McGrath remembered. "The concept has been around ever since there were different tribes with different rites and rituals thousands of years ago. In Richland, I brought Chief Wilson Charley to class and took the students to the river to meet the Celilo and Yakima. In Europe, we opened the eyes of American kids—raised on Coca-Cola and hamburgers—to the cultures of France, Italy, and Germany, and in Santa Fe at the institute we introduced Indians to Picasso, Matisse, and modernism. The genuinely multicultural goes all ways, not one way, and, if it's good for some, it ought to be good for all."

"Art is a planet," McGrath told teachers, students, and administrators. He preferred to use that phrase—it was another of his mantras—than to harp on multiculturalism; "isms" usually didn't go over well in the classroom. Borrowing one of his favorite lines from one of his favorite movies, *The Wizard of Oz*, and tweaking it, too, he would say to American teachers from Massachusetts, California, Ohio, Kansas, and elsewhere, "We're not in Kansas anymore. We're in Asia. Make the best of it and the most of it in the classroom."

Teaching an Asian culture—whether it was Japanese, Korean, Okinawan, or Filipino—to teachers and students was a tall order. Now and then, McGrath met resistance. Some American teachers in Manila, Seoul, and Tokyo insisted on doing things exactly the same way they did them in Boston, Chicago, and Kansas City. Moreover, on one occasion, he met opposition from an American minister at a military base in Seoul, Korea, where the students made a mural with images of Asian Zodiac animals. The minister complained that the mural was neither Christian nor American and was sacrilegious. The school principal agreed, and it was destroyed.

For a year, McGrath took a much-needed break from Asia, returned to the states, and taught on the Hopi reservation in Arizona. His time in Arizona, teaching Indians again, reminded him how different the states were, and that experience helped him appreciate the dilemma that many of the American students faced in Asia. They were Americans, but they didn't know their own cultures and hadn't been exposed to the diversity of America itself.

Most of their lives were spent on military bases in the midst of military personnel, surrounded by the culture of the military, with guns, uniforms, ranks, regiments, and men and women marching in formation. Many of the students were also lonely and homesick; they had not chosen to be in Japan or the Philippines; they felt as though their parents had dragged them off. They wanted to go home, be with normal American kids, eat normal food, and watch normal American TV.

Back in Asia again and with homesick students in mind, McGrath packed into classrooms as much of the heft and richness of America as he could pack. It was an America, of course, of his own choosing which meant that he often taught students about American Indians,

American dances, folk art, storytelling, woodcarving, and juggling. Midway through his time in Asia, he started an artist-in-residence program in the schools and imported American artists, including his friend and former colleague from IAIA, Charles Loloma, who was the first living American artist—and the first American Indian as well—the students met. Charles charmed them, told them stories, and had them laughing.

McGrath also brought to Asia—and found funds in the military coffers to pay—a host of creative spirits: Willa Schneberg, a poet from Massachusetts; Daryl Howard, a printmaker from Texas; John Hoover, a wood-carver from Alaska; and Irene Oliver-Lewis, from New Mexico, who knew the stage and who taught improvisational theater. He also brought into the schools two modern dancers from Utah—Jacque Lynn Bell and Julius Lee Prater. From Ashville, North Carolina, came the storytellers Barbara Freeman and Connie Regan. While the logistics felt overwhelming at times, the results made the effort worthwhile.

133

Sometimes the artist-in-residence experienced culture shock. Oliver-Lewis was born and raised in New Mexico and educated at New Mexico State. She had never been far from home, and in Japan she was suddenly in the midst of a culture she didn't know or understand. "When I arrived I said to myself, 'Oh, my gosh, what have I done"? she explained. Then she asked another question, "What can I possibly offer these people"? McGrath suggested that she be herself, make her own art, and share what she knew from her own experiences.

"After meeting and talking with Jim, I relaxed," Oliver-Lewis said. "I did a workshop for blind people. In the process, I learned to trust myself as an artist and came to appreciate the importance of opening up and revealing yourself, not only in your own culture but in other cultures, too. Opening up can be a challenge, but it's often necessary for real learning to take place."

Like many isms, multiculturalism had its foes in government, on local school boards, and in teachers' unions. Some teachers, administrators, and parents did all they could to prevent it from entering the curriculum, and they depicted it as noxious. It was "reverse racism," some said, a position that McGrath found irritating. The anti-multicultural forces, he argued, simply didn't want to surrender old ways that had worked for years—or hadn't.

The anti-multicultural ideologues, McGrath argued, were afraid that U.S. national identity would be diluted and diffused by adding different cultures to the mix. But multiculturalism was too powerful to keep out of schools; it had a logic of its own and a momentum of its own, too.

134

For McGrath, multiculturalism reflected the social transformations taking place in the United States: the arrival of Central and South America immigrants who spoke Spanish and were shaped by Latin American culture, and the rush of immigrants from Asia who spoke dozens of different languages, from Mandarin Chinese to Japanese, Korean, and Filipino—the very same languages that McGrath heard in Asia. America began to look more and more like the whole planet, and that shift filled him with a sense of possibilities and opportunities.

To teach teachers who would teach their students the lessons of diversity, McGrath devised dozens of exercises. One called on teachers to make real hats that they could wear and take home and that reflected the cultures of the world. McGrath provided the materials and the tools: scissors, feathers, glue, cloth, and paper. The teachers provided their imaginations; a main point

of the exercise was to show the importance of listening
and following directions. Another exercise called on participants to take the first letters of their names—like
J.A.M. for James Arthur McGrath—and use them to
tell a story. It was a useful way to teach the alphabet to
young students, he discovered, and a way to fire creativity, too, from very simple beginnings.

Yet another exercise called for a student in a physical
education class to stretch out on a piece of paper on the
floor and for another student to trace the outline of his
or her body. This exercise brought art into the gym and
encouraged students to be aware of their own bodies,
whether at rest or in motion. Lying on the paper, a boy
or girl might move his or her arms and legs to illustrate
a jump shot in basketball, for example. In a biology
class, the students molded clay into the shape of the
frogs they were studying, or else they traced the outline
of a vital organ in the human body—a brain, a stomach,
and a heart—and learned human anatomy through art.

One of McGrath's favorite exercises involved puppets
that teachers and students made with their own hands.
A puppet might be Cinderella, the Buddha, George Washington, a family member, or classmate. The students
would take on the identity of the puppet that they made
and tell a story about it.

As if those exercises weren't enough to generate creativity, McGrath also published a yearly journal entitled
Sun, which included poems, drawings, and sketches
from students and teachers. The name of the publication
was a way to pay homage to Japanese culture and to the
sacred place of the Sun itself as the source of life. The
motto for the publication—"Contact is the appreciation
of differences"—came from the German-born American
experimental psychologist and father of gestalt therapy,

Fritz Perls, whose life and work McGrath discovered in
the 1970s and whose ideas about education he incorporated into his teaching.

Sun number one appeared in 1975. McGrath edited
it and designed it. Michael Puskas, the coordinator for
the language arts, assisted him. The last *Sun* for which
McGrath was responsible appeared in 1985. In ten
years, he published the artwork of 3,774 students and
staff members in the Department of Defense's overseas
schools. Read the names of the students who contributed
to the *Sun*, and their rich cultural and ethnic heritage
leaps out from the pages: Toni Smith, Jasmin Celebcigil,
Kathy McCoy, Gloria Jackson, Marian Muszynski,
Young Sanchez, Laura Zung, James Ziedzic, Frances
Ku, and Glenn Gunderson. No teachers had to leave the
classroom to experience multiculturalism. It was right
there in the flesh.

Some of the student art depicted guns and bombs.
But much of it was anti-war; one sketch depicted a
soldier in uniform lying still on the ground, his eyes
closed, at peace with himself and the world around
him. McGrath included everything and anything. In
the introduction to the first issue of *Sun*, he wrote,
"These freshly conceived worlds are beautiful because
they are real and new as the first created suns that
they are."

The students wrote *haiku* in Japanese as well as in
English about the environments that surrounded them.
Again and again they returned to the knot of their own
personal identities. One sixteen-year-old girl wrote, "I
am not you. I am not her. I am not him. I am ME." She
spoke for classmates who were learning what made them
individuals apart from the crowd. Now and then, adults
also submitted work to *Sun*. In one poem that McGrath

published, a teacher wrote that her students were "frustrating" and that they also caused her "to wonder" about the world.

McGrath was especially proud of *Sun* and proud, too, of an Intercultural Arts Summer Program that took place in the Philippines where American teachers and Filipino artists danced, acted, made art, played music, cooked, and ate together.

"It was a scene of the most adventurous creativity that I have ever been involved in," McGrath wrote in his assessment of the program. He also raved about two summer workshops that he created with the special education coordinator, Dorothy Seavy, for disabled children, held in the mountains of the Philippines. From the Department of Defense's schools all across Asia came children who were deaf, blind, physically handicapped, as well as those afflicted with Down's syndrome.

137

"The arts experience will help the handicapped to understand themselves and the world in which they live," McGrath wrote in the brochure for the program. There were forty-eight different workshops in music, dance, film, and the visual arts, and there was cooking, eating, and story telling. It was a success because of the assistance of many others, such as Ricardo Carrasco, who worked in a Manila center for Down's syndrome and who brought together Filipinos and Americans.

Magic tricks were not necessary to create workshops and conferences, McGrath discovered, but some strategies were more effective than others. "It helps to start with the recognition that deep down everyone has a gift or a talent they want to give to the world," he said. "People want to do things that make them joyous. I created environments where they could express themselves creatively whether it was cooking or making bonsai. Of course, it helped to be in tune to local cultures. It always does. The local ought to inform a school's curriculum. I learned that lesson at my first teaching position, and I carried it with me to Europe, New Mexico, and Asia."

IV. Stranger in a Strange Land

Joan and Tom Rudholm, a husband and wife from California, worked with McGrath at workshops for the disabled. Beginning in 1967, they taught at schools for the children of military personnel and continued to teach in Asia until 1988. Working on Clark Air Force base in the Philippines, they saw a constant flow of troops back and forth from Vietnam, and they saw POWs after they were released from captivity in North Vietnam.

"Teachers often provided the only real source of stability for the students," Joan Rudholm said. "Their parents were in and out of combat. The turnover of the student population was tremendous; when a parent's tour of duty was over, the child was pulled out of school. Sometimes by the end of a semester there was a big batch of students that was totally new and different from the batch that began the semester."

At the height of the war in Vietnam, the schools were overcrowded, and there were double sessions to accommodate all of them. The first session began at 6:30 a.m. and ended at noon; the second ran from 12:30 p.m. to 6 p.m. "The war was the backdrop to all our teaching," Tom Rudholm remembered. "It went on and on for years."

Joan explained, "One of the main lessons we learned from McGrath was how to work with other people, how to stay focused and not get caught up in ego." She added,

"McGrath was like the main character in Robert Hein-lein's novel, *Stranger in a Strange Land.* He fell in love with everyone. He saw each and everyone in a holistic way, and he saw the beauty in everybody and pulled it out of people."

Joan also noted that Jim had an explosive temper. He was only human after all. Tom agreed with Joan on the subject of McGrath's temper, but he added that he also had patience and excelled in the realm of the multi-cultural. "The festivals for the disabled were intensely emotional experiences," Tom remembered. "I would just break down and cry at the sight of those blind and deaf students as they arrived in the Philippines and went to work making art."

In Asia, McGrath was usually too involved in day-to-day activities to write. But occasionally he crafted an essay and gave a talk. In a 1976 article, entitled "Where Do I Begin to Say the Things I Want to Say," for the magazine, *Smashing Ideas*, he noted that the "creative capacities in students are smothered and repressed at an early age."

139

That realization prompted him to redouble his efforts. There was a "spark of creativity" in each and everyone, he explained. "Everything is Possible," he insisted, capitalizing the "P" for added emphasis. His role, and the role of all teachers, he explained, was to turn little sparks into blazes of creativity. "We're responsible not to let the creative spark be smothered," he said.

V. Simplify

In 1982, he was the keynote speaker at a conference of the United States Society for Education Through the

Arts (USSEA) in Los Angeles that was coordinated by Dr. Paul Kravagna of California State University at Northridge. In his formal remarks, McGrath was more critical than ever before of American society and American behavior, too, especially the American habit, as he saw it, of "rushing in, offering aid, and leaving before the recipient even knows what it means."

In the clash between industrial cultures and aboriginal cultures, his allegiance was to the aboriginals, he explained. He looked back at his teaching experience in Richland, Washington, next door to Hanford where plutonium was manufactured and where there was a high rate of cancer. "Families were getting their daily doses of radiation," he said. "If I were in Columbia High School now, I would talk about radiation, and I would ask students to design anti-nuclear posters. I would integrate consciousness about nuclear issues into art."

140

In the 1982 talk he delivered to art teachers, he made practical suggestions and offered specific lessons. He suggested that teachers "really listen," "create community-centered schools" and cross-cultural, intellectual, geographical, and political boundaries.

"I'm learning to simplify my life and work so that I can teach students and teachers to simplify," he said at the conclusion of his keynote address. At times, he was elegiac, transcendental, and inspiring. "I am not fixed in space or time," he explained. "I am anchored in the stars, and I am webbed about the Earth."

CHAPTER EIGHT
Risks and Rewards
of Teaching Art

I. From Albuquerque to Zuni

A fter a dozen years in Asia, McGrath returned to Santa Fe and found that now more than ever before it was a tourist destination and an American art capital. In Santa Fe, there were more artists and galleries than ever before. "When I left there were five galleries," he remembered. "In the mid-1980s, that number jumped to 205." And yet there was no longer a gallery where James could hang his paintings and exhibit his sculptures. Out of the country—and away from the commercial U.S. art scene—for a dozen years, the gallery that once exhibited his work dropped him for newer talent close to home. For a time, he was lost and knew that he had to reinvent himself if he was to carry on as an artist.

"My friend, Mary Lou Denning, who had worked with me in Europe in the 1960s and again at the IAIA in the 1970s, warned me how difficult it would be for me to fit in again in the Santa Fe art world. She knew many of the painters and the gallery owners, and she was right." St. John's College in Santa Fe provided space for his work, but he found that he had to venture outside traditional channels to secure new spaces where he could exhibit his sketches and drawings.

The twelve years in Asia changed him, as well as his art and his vision of the world, and it took time, energy, and imagination to integrate and channel the changes into new modes of expression. Initially, McGrath felt a sense of frustration. "Mary Lou empathized with me," he said. "She helped me come through that difficult period."

It took months to unpack the ceramics and tools he brought back from Asia and years to unpack the attitudes and feelings he had absorbed. It was a time to settle down again, to write letters and to call his daughters who were now young women, and to spend time with friends.

"I continued many of the customs and rituals I learned in Japan," he said. "I always bought beautiful freshcut flowers in Santa Fe and arranged them at home. I carried on the Japanese tea ceremony with Cynthia West, a fellow poet." As his energy returned and as he felt increasingly settled in his own home, he returned to the roots of his own art and grounded himself in the land itself. "I walked in the fields behind my house, picked up stones, and etched them in the Okinawan style," he said. "Then, too, I did brush and ink work in the Chinese manner that I learned in Asia and exhibited much of it at the Yummy Café, a Chinese restaurant, in Santa Fe." Now, in hindsight, he could see that, as he put it, Asian life and culture had touched his "inner soul." What he once regarded as a "foreign culture" had become over the years an integral part of him, and so it felt natural to express himself with Chinese brush and ink.

McGrath was itchy to secure a foothold in the classroom and teach art again. He'd taught all the arts at
Columbia High School, but that was in the 1950s. He'd
taught painting to students at IAIA, but that was in the
1960s. For the past thirty years, he'd been an administrator and a teacher of art teachers, not an instructor
of grade school boys and girls. "Why do you want to
teach elementary school kids again"? he was asked at
job interviews. "Because I can bring out their creativity,"
he would say. "Because I wanted to inspire students,
and because I know they all have art within them that's
aching to be expressed."

He applied to be an artist-in-residence for a new
program housed in the New Mexico Office of Cultural
Affairs, but much to his disappointment he was turned
down. So he applied again and this time was accepted.
Lara Morrow, the executive director, had worked for the
National Endowment for the Arts in Washington, D.C.,
and she recognized McGrath as a rare talent not to be
lost. A native of California and graduate of the University
of Oregon at Eugene, she hired him and put him to work.

143

"I believed then as I believe now in creativity and in
creating the conditions for creativity," Morrow said. "In
the classroom, doing things creatively helps build self-
confidence. McGrath was all about making creativity
happen spontaneously and by design as well. He knew
how to bond with people and how to make them feel safe.
He had loads of patience, and he listened to people, all
of which came in handy when he taught in the public
schools in New Mexico."

As an artist-in-residence, McGrath traveled to public
schools around the state. He did not have as large a territory to cover as he'd had in Europe and in Asia, but he
put a lot of mileage on his car driving from Santa Fe to

Albuquerque and to Zuni and to more than half-dozen
places with magical names such as Alamogordo, Mescalero, and Tularosa.

In the elementary school in Tularosa, with the support of the art teacher, Sandra Weber, he taught fifth
and sixth graders to work in bronze, though skeptical
educators said that just couldn't be done. Fifth and sixth
graders were too young, too small, and inexperienced
to work with an adult medium like bronze, McGrath
was told. He went ahead with the project and the students—who were both Anglos and Indians from the
Apache reservation—made art that delighted him, their
parents, and the dubious administrators who said it
just couldn't be done. The bronze-cast animals that his
Tularosa students created were installed on stones in a
park on the school grounds, and they became a destination for the community.

At Tularosa, McGrath taught writing, weaving, and
sculpting. He provided workshops for teachers, super-
vised the students who made murals, and created cur-
ricula that integrated the arts and the sciences. Whole
families came to his workshops, and grandmothers
worked along side their grandchildren. Teaching across
the generations appealed to him as much as teaching
across cultures. McGrath didn't have a blueprint for
success, but he had been doing what he did for so many
decades that at Tularosa he knew what to do and how to
do it instinctively.

"Art is all around us," he told students and parents.
"It's not just on a wall in a museum." He had been saying
much the same thing for years, but it was still news, and
it helped young students who were often intimidated by
the idea of art and thought of artists as weird creatures
from another planet.

McGrath persuaded communities that they wanted
and needed art, even though they didn't realize it themselves. Once they started to make art, it was difficult
to stop them, and they wondered how they had managed to live so long without it. Part of the challenge
McGrath faced, after so many years of teaching, was
how to remain fresh and how not to become stale. Fortunately, there were always new challenges. Almost all
the elementary schools in the towns and villages under
his purview did not have art teachers; his mission was to
persuade instructors in all subjects to recognize that art
was essential to the entire school, and that it could bring
out the very best in students.

In the 1990s, he worked on an arts-in-the-classroom
project sponsored by the New Mexico Arts Division. One
of the team members, Irene Oliver-Lewis, had been an
artist-in-residence in Asia when McGrath was the arts
and humanities coordinator for the American schools
on military bases. Now she was back in New Mexico.
Together, she and McGrath taught workshops for teachers on the campus of the University of New Mexico in
Albuquerque. "Our workshops were multicultural," she
said. "We included cowboy culture along with Hispanic
and Native American culture. We did original theatrical
performances, and we involved the teachers. We thought
it was essential that they do the same things that they
required of their students."

II. Nest and Anchor

Traveling about New Mexico would not have been
as pleasant for McGrath if he had not had a real home
where he could retreat, regroup, and unwind. Teachers

don't just exist in front of students in the classroom, McGrath would say. They needed space and time to be alone. Even when he didn't travel far—when he gave workshops in Santa Fe at the Georgia O'Keeffe Museum and the Children's Museum—he appreciated the fact that he could sleep in his own bed and make coffee in the morning in his own kitchen while his cats, Ruff and Tumble, rubbed their backs against his legs.

In 1971, at the age of forty three, he had the foresight to buy eight acres of land in Cieneguilla, on the outskirts of Santa Fe, that came with a decrepit building that was once a stagecoach stop. In 1973, McGrath added a new roof to protect it from snow, rain, and sun, but the structure had no floor, doors, windows, electricity, and no running water. To make it habitable, he worked with a crew for nearly a year and was reminded that as a boy he had worked alongside his father. He remembered, too, how hard physical labor could be and not any easier now that he was fifty years old.

146

When the house was completed, with fireplaces in every room and the space he needed to store his art, he had a real home—a "nest" and an "anchor," he would say. He came to see it as "the center around which I move" and as "a sacred place." He gave workshops in writing and painting, and there were readings in his apple orchard along the river. Lee Udall came and cooked for the students. As always teaching nurtured him, and as always teaching was not enough to satisfy his emotional wants and needs. His life stretched beyond the classroom and outside the school.

At Thanksgiving, McGrath invited friends, former students, and fellow teachers to a feast. There were

Anglos and Indians and food from several cultures: turkey with stuffing, roast elk, sweet potatoes, peas, and wild mushroom soup. For desert there was pumpkin pie and coffee. Guests would sit on pillows on the floor, eat, write, and make pictures with crayons. "I'm happy," McGrath wrote to his daughters. "On festive occasions like Thanksgiving with food and friends, it feels like the circle is complete. Almost, but not quite."

III. Nation at Risk

McGrath found that American schools had changed yet again and not always for the better. In the world of education, he heard grumblings and rumblings, perhaps more than ever before in the twentieth century in the United States. A long list of complaints echoed around the country: students didn't study anymore; they graduated from high schools unprepared for college or the work place. Those were the stark conclusions outlined in a report issued by the National Commission on Excellence in Education created in 1981 by T. H. Bell, Ronald Reagan's secretary of education. The report, published in 1983 and entitled *A Nation at Risk: The Imperative for Educational Reform*, painted a dire picture of the American public school system, and private schools and parochial schools, too.

McGrath read the report and mulled over the recommendations: more stringent requirements for high school students; four years of English; three years of math; three years of science; and one-and-a-half years of computer science. In the years ahead, computer science would grow by leaps and bounds; students would spend hours at their computers, whether required or not.

McGrath would not be swept up in the computer craze. He didn't buy one or use one. He used a landline—he didn't have a cell phone—and he went on writing letters the old-fashioned way and sent them through the postal service. In Japan, he had tried to boot up and get online and had failed. "I didn't have the mind for it," he said. "I never could type; typing was the only class I ever failed—in junior high school in Tacoma."

His education at Lincoln High School looked like a model that might be emulated. McGrath had four years of English, three years of math, two years of science, three years of music, and he could converse in French. His teachers had high expectations of him and all their students. What he had learned in high school was now, in many cases, what students learned at college.

148   In *A Nation at Risk*, in an italicized sentence that leapt out at McGrath, the authors called for *"more rigorous and measurable standards and higher expectations for academic performance and student conduct."* The era of testing, testing, and more testing had begun with a bang. It would accelerate under George Bush after he became president in 2000 and promulgated the slogan, "No Child Left Behind."

Testing was the cornerstone of the recommendations for "reform" that were made by the National Commission on Excellence in Education, though it also called for other changes: increases in teacher salaries; more rigorous standards for teachers; and proof that instructors had an "aptitude" for teaching. If these reforms were put in place, and if Americans understood that it was "patriotic" to support education, then the American school system might be saved, and citizens might become lifelong learners. That was the hope.

IV. Rafael Gonzales: Seeing With the Heart

Soon after he returned to the states, McGrath
went to work at the College of Santa Fe where Anglo,
Hispanic, and Indian students sat side-by-side without
coming to blows and even collaborated on projects. The
school boasted about its ethnic diversity, and there was
also a mix of older and younger students. McGrath
taught painting, sculpture, and a course for undergrad-
uates who wanted to teach art, but he was often disappointed and downbeat.

"Standards did get lost," he said. "Many of the students in my classes were lackadaisical. They didn't take
classes seriously, and they had a difficult time finish-
ing projects that they started. They complained about
exams, and they had a false sense of sophistication.
They were awfully laidback."

149

McGrath's complaints reflected a growing unease
among American teachers at the end of the twentieth
century. "Students lived in the superficiality of the now
and didn't have deeper roots," he observed, as did many
of his colleagues. " Students knew about computer programs, who was playing for the Yankees, and what the
topic of conversation was on the Tonight Show, but they
didn't know about Faulkner, Joan Miró, Gertrude Stein,
history, geography, and American Indians. Our society
overemphasizes youth, fails to see the value of older people and neglects deeper, invisible kinds of beauty. Then,
too, it often ignores the beauty of the natural world, such
as the desert of New Mexico."

At the College of Santa Fe—a school that traced its
roots back to 1859 and that offered a program in the creative arts—Richard Cook, the head of the arts division,
hired McGrath as though he were hiring a teaching leg-

end. It was McGrath's first real experience as a teacher in a private school. One of the students Cook wanted McGrath to reach, teach, and rescue was Rafael Gonzales, a Vietnam veteran who was wounded in combat and who was going blind. Shrapnel hit him in the eyes. The degeneration of his vision was slow and steady; objects became blurred and outlines indistinct.

Growing up in Albuquerque in a family of ten brothers and sisters, Gonzales had difficulty expressing himself verbally, but he could always express himself with line, shape, and color—until he went into the military, and then, as he explained, "art went out the window." When he came back to New Mexico from Vietnam, he turned to art again for his sanity and salvation. He knew instinctively that art would help where nothing else could.

"Rafael looked like he could have been in a gang in L.A.," McGrath remembered. "He was at risk in many ways, but beneath that rough, tough exterior he had a gentle soul and the spirit of an artist."

Unlike many of his classmates, there was nothing lackadaisical about him; he took classes seriously and he devoted himself to his art. It was a matter of survival. "I was ready for McGrath when he came along," Rafael remembered. "He taught me that reality is not as real as it seems to be and that it's only as real as you see it. I learned from McGrath that art has to come from your heart and soul and that it's not about copying, but about interpreting."

At the College of Santa Fe, Rafael made a large alabaster butterfly that impressed McGrath greatly and a sculpture he called "After the War" that became a part of the Vietnam Veterans Memorial in Albuquerque. Art was Rafael's therapy and enabled him to heal emotional wounds, though it did not save his eyesight.

"When I could no longer see with my eyes, I learned to see with my heart," he said. "It was an amazing discovery for me personally and for the art I made."

V. The Return of the Richland Three

Rafael Gonzales would have fit into the company of McGrath's outstanding students from Columbia High School in Richland, Washington. For thirty years, his "A" students stayed in touch, wrote letters, invited him to their openings at art galleries, and sent examples of their work. They had bonded at Richland, and the bond had never been broken. While they each went off in their own separate directions, they also continued the arc that they started at Richland, and they always looked back and paid homage to McGrath, the pilgrim who showed them the way to make art in their own individual ways.

McGrath's Richland students were an apt illustration of American education at his best. They also showed that gains might be made when a teacher took risks, as McGrath had done. Indeed, teaching had always been a big risk for him because he had stuttered and was told not to teach by his own instructors. He took risks with his Richland students, giving them, for example, the key to the art department so they could let themselves in and out and have their own studio to work as long, as late, and as hard as they wanted.

All teaching inevitably involved the taking of risks, McGrath believed, and he never stopped taking them. Risks led to rewards. A risk wasn't simply or only an invitation to danger, disaster, and loss. Taking a risk could provide an opportunity for growth, discovery, and illumination—for those moments when the creator stood back, looked at work done, and said, "WOW!"

While there never was and never would be a McGrath School of Thought or School of Art, there were certain abiding approaches: respect for the process of creation; willingness to go creatively where one had never been before; and a belief in oneself and one's individual vision. The exceptional students from Columbia High School embodied those qualities whether they worked in film, such as Dorothy Dowis and John Haugse; or in architecture, such as Jim Scoggin; or in poetry, such as Bill Witherup.

Then there was the protean band of brothers— William Allan, William Wiley, and Bob Hudson—who worked in several media, often at the same time.

152

VI. William Allan: Fishing for Art

Allan was the oldest of the three and the most outgoing. After Richland, he attended and then graduated in 1958 from the California School of Fine Arts in San Francisco with a B.F.A. It took years before he found himself as an artist—perhaps longer than it took Hudson or Wiley—but once he did find himself, he painted in a variety of styles: realistic, surrealistic, whimsical, and symbolic, always with meticulous attention to detail, whether it was the scales on a fish or an article of clothing.

Sometimes his work looked like it was commissioned for an ad, or at least a mock ad. Sometimes there were autobiographical references, as in a large oil painting entitled "The Transient Poet Leaving Home," which went through several versions as though he had to work out his theme again and again until it was out of his system. In "Transient Poet Leaving Home I," a stick figure carries a pack of cigarettes in one hand and a matchbook with one solitary match in another. In the background, there's a dark house; a lightening storm electrifies the ominous night sky.

"It's about myself, my experience, and the experience of many young kids as they grow up," Allan explained. "It's about being one's own self and not the child of a father or a mother because as an artist you have to invent yourself and be yourself." In another signature work, entitled "Shadow Repair for the Western Man," from 1970, jeans and shoes hover above a snow-capped mountain range. There's no man in the jeans, and the absence of a man suggests the disappearance of "Western Man" and a commentary on western civilization itself.

153

Allan never stopped exploring, experimenting, and breaking new ground. He went his own way; painted fish and learned about the painting of fish by fishing in streams and lakes. Mostly, he didn't worry about who would buy his art or where he would sell it. When he did find himself thinking about how to market a painting before he had finished it, he brought himself back to the work itself and paid attention to the process of creation. Painting itself was a kind of fishing, he realized. It took patience before an idea nibbled at his imagination and then tugged at the end of the line. Art and fishing both called for catching. In art you caught an idea, a color, a shape, and went with it.

"Adventure—intense personal adventure—is essential for me as an artist," Allan said. "Painting keeps me alive and vital. I have never been interested in developing talent; that's boring. You have to need art in order to develop art and become a genuine artist. You have to have a sense of discovery and to trust the creative process. For me, there's always been the dialectic between that joy in the exploration itself and the anxiety of not knowing where you're going."

VII. Bob Hudson: Junk Into Art

Bob Hudson was the youngest member of the band of brothers. Of the three men, he came from the family who lived closest to poverty but who enjoyed the riches of the landscape. For a time, the whole family —mom, dad, and Bob—scavenged along the sides of roads for empty soda pop bottles and, at the nearest store, collected the deposit, then bought milk, sugar, eggs, and coffee. Bob remembered when he and his family lived on rabbit hash; his father hunted and came home with supper. His mother cooked in a skillet in the trailer they rented. In high school, Bob worked on a tugboat on the Columbia River, taking barges down to Portland, and in summers he drove trucks filled with wheat after it was harvested. If it weren't for McGrath, Bob would say, he'd have grown up to become the captain of a tugboat.

As a teenager, Picasso was Hudson's favorite artist; he wanted to meet Picasso, and he was sorry he never had the opportunity to watch him in his studio. He read everything he could about Picasso and collected every book that contained Picasso's work. But he took his inspiration as much from nature as from other artists. Indeed, Hudson was profoundly influenced by the Columbia River, the Yakima Indians, and the desert of eastern Washington. Sagebrush got under his skin and he craved it. He'd get into his car and drive hours until

he arrived in the desert; then he knew he was at home.
Cities didn't feel comfortable to him, though he spent
six years at the San Francisco Institute of Fine Art
from 1957 to 1963, rooming with Allan and Wiley and
befriending Manuel Neary and Joan Brown, one of the
few women artists at the institute who combined in her
own personal style of living feminine sophistication and
glamour with a male kind of camaraderie.

Hudson also met Ansel Adams, Richard Diebenkorn,
and Willem de Kooning, and in the midst of the creative cauldron of San Francisco in the 1960s, his own
imagination caught fire. At the Institute of Fine Arts,
he made sculptures with steel, then painted them bright
colors, which shocked teachers who shook their heads in
disapproval. His first show—with Wiley at the Green
Street Gallery in San Francisco—was a success and
from the start the critics paid attention to him.

155

Hudson would often work on three, four, and five
pieces at the same time. In a huge studio, which looked
like a machine shop and a garage, he stored all the
debris that he gathered from junkyards and at the
ocean. He found a place in his art for the things most
people tossed away. McGrath had taught him that art
was everywhere and that everything might be art.
Hudson carried that idea to its logical conclusion and
made art from split wood, veils from women's hats,
feathers, rusty axes, old dictionaries, bent fenders from
cars and trucks, and much, much more. On his property, he had porcelain sinks, farm implements, and all
shapes of iron and steel that he welded together into big
pieces—"visual contradictions," one critic called them.

He worked with his hands and with tools and
machines; some of his art required hard physical labor
and the lifting of heavy pieces, as well as hammering

and sawing. He dreamed and almost hallucinated, too, without the benefit of drugs. Hudson always saw more than what was on the surface. He had a real sweetness about him and innocence, too, though he was also savvy about the market and knew how to talk to agents, dealers, and gallery owners.

VIII. Wily Wiley: Funky Zen Punster

Bill Wiley was the most productive artist in the band of brothers. He practically lived in his studio—though he came out for air, meals, and for exhibits of his work which took place all over the United States and in Europe. His first art exhibit was in 1960 when he was a student at the San Francisco School of Fine Arts where faculty members weren't sure what to make of him because he didn't have a single style.

The German-born art critic, Peter Selz, curated Wiley's first museum show at the University Art Museum at the University of California, Berkeley, in 1967 and applied the word "funk" to describe it. "The casual, irreverent, insincere California atmosphere, with its absurd elements—weather, clothes, 'skinny-dipping,' hobby craft, sun-drenched mentality, Doggie Diner, perfumed tissue, do-it-yourself—all this drives the artist's vision inward," Selz wrote in an essay published in *Art in a Turbulent Era.* He added, "This is the Land of Funk."

Wiley was funky, whimsical, and overtly political. He couldn't keep politics and topical issues out of his art—which endeared him to Selz. He almost always made a statement about war, pollution, global warming, lies, greed, and more, and he continually made visual

jokes in his paintings and sketches. He loved puns and
he combined images and words on canvases, a style he'd
developed at Richland where almost all of his classmates
recognized his immense talents and expected him to
grow up and to become a renowned artist. He didn't
disappoint anyone unless it was perhaps himself. Wiley
seemed to be relaxed and a Zen master, but beneath the
calm exterior one might find anxieties that drove him to
be all the more creative. He could imitate all the European masters and did, from Bruegel to Rembrandt. He
was a consummate post-modern artist.

Born in Indiana in 1937, Wiley grew up on the
road. He bounded about the West with his mother and
father, who searched relentlessly for work and a business to run. Sitting in the back seat of the family car
with his brother, Bill Wiley read, drew, and surrounded
himself with his own imaginary worlds. In the books he
157
devoured as a boy, he loved the drawings in which there
were hidden animals, and, as an adult, he retained a
child-like delight in secrets, coded messages, and images
half-buried on the canvas. You could stand in front of
one of Wiley's large canvases, gaze at it for an hour
or more, notice all sorts of little details, and see, too,
that one part of the painting offered a commentary on
another part. Wiley was his own best critic.

Perhaps the contemporary American writer with
whom he felt the closest affinity was Kurt Vonnegut,
the novelist who wrote weirdly comic novels, like *Cat's
Cradle*, about the end of the world. Wiley was apoca-
lyptic and saw humor in the apocalypse, though he also
meant to wake up the whole country and prod, shame,
and cajole America into saving itself, its air, water,
and earth. Not surprisingly, he admired the surreal-
ists—Salvador Dali, Giorgio de Chirico, and especially

Marcel Duchamp. He morphed throughout his career.

Wiley's big breakthrough came about in the East in 1967 and 1968, when New York seemed like the center of the known universe and from all over the country creative souls drifted into Manhattan, Brooklyn, and Queens to make art, play rock 'n' roll, and join the American cultural revolution.

For a time in the early 1960s, Wiley thought that his career as an artist had come to an end, and he didn't know where to turn. "Then I decided I was just gonna do what I wanted to do and see where it would take me," he remembered. That was a lesson that he'd also learned from McGrath—to surrender to the creative process itself, have faith that one would make discoveries along the way, and emerge with a new vision.

158

Wiley came back to California from the East Coast, settled in the San Geronimo Valley in Marin County which he loved for its landscapes, remoteness, and serenity. As soon as he could make a living from art, he stopped teaching, though he didn't forget the lessons he learned in McGrath's classroom.

"Way back in high school, McGrath gave me sophisticated ideas of what being an artist might be like," Wiley said. "Because of him, becoming an artist seemed like something I could actually achieve. I knew that I might really grow up and paint." And so he did. Hudson and Allan grew up and became artists, too. Having students such as Wiley, Hudson, and Allan helped to make teaching worthwhile.

McGrath's former Richland students launched an event entitled "An Evening in Honor of James McGrath," held at the San Francisco Museum of Modern Art, one of the premiere venues for art in the Bay Area. McGrath had a hefty resume and a long list of achievements, but in the art world Wiley, Hudson, and Allan were better known than he was, and it was their fame that brought him into the spotlight.

"An Evening in Honor of James McGrath" was both a reunion and a coming-out party for McGrath as an artist. It was never a secret that he had taught Allan, Hudson, and Wiley. They acknowledged him in interviews with reporters and in statements about their own art, but this was a public event that disclosed to the world one of the longest running mentoring relationships in American art education. McGrath's ex-wife, Jean, came after years of rancor, and so did his daughters who were in their thirties and proud of their father.

"I do regret not having time with my own family," he said. "But that is another story. I shall be thankful for what I have in each moment and who I am in the time that I have."

At the San Francisco Museum of Modern Art, Hudson and Allan spoke, and there was music by Wiley and his brother. Soon after that event, McGrath returned to San Francisco. At the Commonwealth Club, he gave a slide show and talked about Hudson, Wiley, and Allan, tracing their work from high school days to the present. McGrath also had a major exhibit of his work at the Meridian Gallery in San Francisco that Bill Allan curated with help from Hudson, Wiley, and Jim Scoggin. Kevin Red Star came from Montana, and Columbia High School students such as Aida Mankowski arrived from Canada.

"There was little talk about teaching," McGrath said. "Instead we talked about being artists and the artist's life, and that felt very fulfilling."

CHAPTER NINE

L'Homme de Santa Fe:
Art at Home and Far Way

I. Art is Like a Drum in the Night

The Congolese knew that his name was James McGrath, but they preferred to call him "the Man from Santa Fe," or more precisely, "L'Homme de Santa Fe," since they spoke French and not English. "L'Homme de Santa Fe" had a poetic ring to it that the French-speaking Congolese artists and poets enjoyed. The strange visitor from New Mexico didn't act like the Americans they read about in books, such as *The Ugly American*, or like John Wayne in the American westerns they watched on movie screens.

In the Congo in 1995, McGrath talked a great deal about New Mexico, its art, culture, and indigenous population. He made New Mexico sound fantastic, and so the Congolese fell in love with New Mexico sight unseen. In an article about McGrath that was entitled "Art Is Like a Drum in the Night" for *La Semaine Africaine*, Marie-Leontine Tsibinda—a Congolese writer—described "L'Homme de Santa Fe" as an American painter who had discovered and fallen in love with traditional Indian arts in New Mexico and had chosen to create his own art in the Southwest.

McGrath had long wanted to travel to Africa. In 1995, at the heart of the continent, he worked with Congolese painters and poets as a visiting artist in an international exchange program sponsored by the United States Information Service (USIS). McGrath was usually upbeat about teaching; superlatives came naturally to him, and he rarely complained about students, their parents, and the community. About the Congo he was especially enthusiastic.

"I met the kindest, gentlest, warmest, most caring, and generous people in the Congo," he wrote at the end of his stay there. "They had so little, and yet their sense of community and family was so intense, real, and alive. I would welcome any of the Congolese artists into my own home, and I would gladly accept another project in the Congo or any other African culture. I was renewed and revitalized there."

161

His experiences in the Congo felt like multiculturalism at its best. Indeed, he had the opportunity to bring Native American arts and traditions to Africa and to take back to New Mexico the arts and the crafts of the Congo. His experience was intensely personal. McGrath's own great-grandparents, whom he had known as a young boy, owned slaves in Tennessee before the Civil War. "Deep down it was hurtful to know that my ancestors owned slaves," he said. "Given the history of slavery, I expected a more hostile reception, or at least a cool reception to me as an American, but there was none of that. The Congolese were sharing; they wanted to make art, and they wanted to work with me."

In the Republic of the Congo, his teaching might

have been a fiasco. When he first arrived, he found that it was vacation, and the students, who were supposed to be enrolled in his workshops, were already at home and wouldn't return any time soon. With help from officials, he recruited artists, all of them adults. Then there was yet another problem: no art supplies. The whole project had to be created and conceived anew, but long experience had taught him to be prepared for mishaps.

In Santa Fe, at the Museum of International Folk Art, he had conducted research on Congolese art and traditions, and in the Congo he put his newfound expertise to work. After he arrived in Brazzaville, he had ample help from the USIS director Tom Doughtery, who had recruited McGrath for the program and who knew about his teaching and his art.

162

Congolese artists also came to the rescue. Marie-Leontine Tsibinda helped to put on an evening of poetry in French, and with McGrath reading in English. Jean Gyldas Ngonhouandou, the official chauffeur, drove McGrath into the jungle where he gathered pigments that were used to make colors. Dieddfonne "Endy" Ndendissa translated from English to French and from French to English. Marcel Foulou and Christian Akouala were the armed guards who protected him. The Congolese artists and poets made James feel at home and appreciated, but tourists were attacked and robbed, and so African men with guns escorted him around Brazzaville and in the surrounding countryside. It took a village to make art, and the whole village of artists came alive with creativity and a sense of joy.

"It wasn't a problem that James was white, because he's an artist and artists are people who are able to live everywhere and be at home everywhere," Marie Tsibinda recalled. "Art is a language that everyone understands,

and the teaching that James did in Brazzaville was
beyond race and nationality."

The Republic of the Congo was an independent
nation, but as McGrath noted, there was a continuing
legacy of colonialism. Overlooking the Congo River, the
luxury hotel where he stayed was off-limits to students.
Then, too, extremes of wealth and poverty were obvious
in Brazzaville. Slums were visible from European-style
mansions hidden behind high walls.

Moreover, at L'Ecole de Peinture de Poto-Poto, the
art school, McGrath found that students were painting,
for the most part, in French and not in Congolese styles.
He aimed to change that as much as possible. Indeed,
the students were soon using indigenous materials and
local motifs they found in masks and textiles. Mostly,
they worked well with one another, though McGrath
noted that occasionally rifts developed around tribal
differences.

163

Classes started at eight in the morning and lasted
until five in the afternoon. McGrath usually went without lunch and so did many of the twenty-two students,
both men and women. He introduced all of them to the
arts of Native Americans and showed the 1976 PBS
series on Indian artists that still seemed new and fresh
to him. So the Congolese saw the work of artists from
the Southwest: R. C. Gorman, Helen Hardin, Fritz
Scholder, and Charles Loloma. The point was not to
paint like Indians or to mimic them, but to make art
from their own culture in the Congo and from contemporary daily life.

McGrath brought his own sculpting tools. Along
the banks of the Congo River, he found a quarry with
beautiful red limestone that was soft enough for carv-
ing and, with help, he transported huge chunks back to

town. The workshops were originally slated to take place inside the American Cultural Center in Brazzaville, but it was too small to accommodate twenty-two students engaged in nearly two dozen projects, all going on at the same time. So the workshops moved to the parking lot. McGrath walked about offering suggestions or just looking. For their final project, the students needed all the room that was available to make twenty-foot-long poles carved with totemic figures that were installed on the grounds of the U.S. Embassy.

From the beginning to the end of the workshop, the Congo River proved to be a great natural resource. He brought the students in Brazzaville to the banks of the Congo, invited them to look at it, touch it, smell it, listen to it, and sketch its ripples, waves, and currents. They had seen it before, of course, but he invited them to look in new ways and see it as though for the first time. The students made a seventy-five-foot mural that offered a visual epic of life on the Congo. Each and everyone also wrote a poem for which McGrath provided the opening words, "I am the River, I..."

McGrath taught a workshop on the business and marketing of art. Most of the artists were already selling their own work and wanted to sell more of it. McGrath suggested that they form a co-op. He also urged them to sell at a low price and make some money rather than at high prices and not sell at all. It would help, too, he told the students, if they put together portfolios of their work to show prospective clients.

At the end of his stay, McGrath launched an exhibit of student work. The expatriate community attended, as did Ambassador and Mrs. Ramsey and Bernard Kolelas, the mayor of Brazzaville. Everyone sold something, and no one went home unhappy. Marie-Leontine Tsibibda noted in her article for *La Semaine Africaine* that "L'Homme de Santa Fe" was a genius at creation and that he had unlocked unknown and unexpected synergies. The students gave a farewell banquet in McGrath's honor at the Poto-Poto art school and served monkey and boa constrictor.

Just before he departed for home, McGrath looked back at his experiences and wrote, "The Congo is a Garden of Eden." Soon afterwards, however, his views changed radically when civil war broke out. War also erupted between Eritrea and Ethiopia, and there was violence in the Cameroon. Multiculturalism could only go so far before it hit deep-seated conflicts. Still, he didn't give up on multiculturalism or the life of the cultural ambassador, and he offered guidelines to Americans who wanted to teach art in Africa.

165

"Do a lot of research ahead of time," he said. "Go to the library and go online. Look at the history and find out about contemporary issues. When you arrive, ask questions in the most respectful way and don't stop asking them. Use your eyes and ears. Be empathetic."

II. On the Edge of Creativity

When he returned to the United States, he began to write poetry everyday. There always had been poetry in his art. Now he wrote poems with renewed vigor and as though his life depended on it. He attended poetry workshops in Ireland and California, learning from Sharon Olds and David Whyte at the Esalen Institute in Big Sur.

"They were both inspiring teachers," he said. "They listened and responded, and they were deeply spiritual." His first really big breakthrough as a writer came about in workshops with Natalie Goldberg, the Santa Fe poet, writer, and author of *Writing Down the Bones*, who encouraged him to write "as if it meant life and death."

As he aged, he became fascinated by the relationship between aging and creativity, much as he had once been fascinated by the relationship between youth and creativity. He coordinated a conference about aging and the making of art in middle and old age. "As I've gotten older I feel more connected with the world," he told a reporter for *Mature Outlook*. "I'm not as worried about sales, money, and making a living as I once was." As he aged, he seemed less defended and less self-protective. He opened up his emotional wounds and used poetry to heal them.

His first book of poetry, which was entitled *At the Edgelessness of Light*, was published in 2005, followed by *Speaking with Magpies* in 2007 and *Dreaming Invisible Voices* in 2009. In the introduction to *At The Edgelessness of Light*, Bill Witherup, who had been a student of McGrath's at Richland and who had grown up to become a poet, described him as "multidexterous … a painter, a poet, and a teacher" and explained that "the poet stimulates the painter, the painter the teacher, the teacher the poet."

Many of his poems are for and about his fellow art teachers and for the administrators who were also his dearest friends: Yvonne Schack from Europe, Betty Taira from Okinawa, Mary Lou Denning from Europe and New Mexico, and Otellie Loloma from IAIA and the Hopi reservation in Arizona. In the poem entitled "At the Edgelessness of Light," he wrote about his first mentor, Paulette Beall. McGrath retrieved memories of his father, mother, Aunt Sinnie, and Uncle Nap who had brought him, when he was a boy, into the world of the American Indian "at the edge of the Newaukum River."

In *Speaking With Magpies*, McGrath wrote about his former students who went on to become poets and artists: Bill Allan, Bill Witherup, Bob Hudson, Donna MacGregor, Bill Wiley, and Dorothy Wiley—and for the artists and poets he met in the Congo. The title poem, "Speaking with Magpies," is for Bill Wiley and suggests that the artist is a kind of magpie who gathers up the shards of the world and turns them into works of art.

Dreaming Invisible Voices is about animals: from ants and elephants to snakes and wolves. "The poems in this book began as a response to the animals of the Asian zodiac calendar while I was living and working in Japan, Korea, Taiwan, Okinawa, and the Philippines," McGrath wrote in the preface to the book. *Dreaming Invisible Voices* is also about making a home and being at home in the world, especially in "House," one of his most evocative poems, which ends

167

> *I am your home.*
> *This is where your heart belongs.*
> *This is where you share your love.*

He had been at home in Richland, Paris, Frankfurt, Tokyo, Seoul, on the Hopi reservation, in Brazzaville, and many other places. Santa Fe was his anchor and his nest where he wrote poems, stored his art, and the art that his friends and students—Otellie Loloma, Kevin Red Star, and others—had given him. Santa Fe was his true home now, and in 2007 Santa Fe named McGrath a "Santa Fe Living Treasure," describing him as "teacher, mentor, instructor, professor, counselor, and guide."

"Painter, sculptor, poet, writer," the notes for the program continued. The list went on and on: "Environmentalist, innovator, advocate, citizen of the world," as though the words "teacher" and "painter" somehow weren't enough. Christine Taylor Patten, who had met McGrath when she was a student and he was a teacher in Germany in 1957, wrote, "James smashed my once blindingly naïve world in one great moment, freeing me forever to see things backwards, upside-down, and to see the world turned inside out."

When a reporter for *The New Mexican* interviewed him about the award, he said, "I believe that we all have a voice and that if someone allows us to speak it, we would have something to say, whether it be in painting or writing or whatever."

"Everything really is possible," McGrath explained one evening in his strange and wonderful house in La Cieneguilla as the magpies flew about and fluttered in the sunlight outside his kitchen window. "We really can learn anything and everything we want to learn. We really can make art, be creative and be sustained by our own communities, here and there, and all around the world."

McGrath was sustained by the achievements of many of his students and colleagues. Irene Oliver-Lewis—the recipient of the New Mexico Governor's Award for Excellence in Education in 2008—was one of the brightest and most energetic of his colleagues. She started Alma d'Arte, a charter school in Las Cruces, New Mexico— her hometown—and with both private and public funding made it a top-notch school in the state.

At Alma d'Arte, seventy percent of the students were Hispanic, twenty-five percent white, about two percent black, and the rest American Indian. Each student chose to follow one of four programs: visual arts, performing arts, culinary arts, and literary arts. "We integrate the arts," Oliver-Lewis said. "We don't just do sequential learning. We emphasize kinesthetic learn-ing—moving about." Some of the underlying reasons for the curriculum were personal, as she explained. "I was dyslexic growing up and had a hard time at school," Oliver-Lewis said. "Then I became involved with the-ater. It changed my life and helped me go on to college and to become a teacher."

As the founder and the executive director of the school, Oliver-Lewis usually didn't teach in the class-room. There were meetings to attend with parents and teachers, forms to sign, and grants to write. But now and then she worked directly with students and applied lessons she learned from McGrath.

"In my school, we look at the strengths people have," Oliver-Lewis said. "We strive to bring out the best in each and every student, and we emphasize the process as much as the product. In workshops I give I empha-size improvisation. The students do monologues and dialogues. I persuade them to relax, use their bodies, voices, and imaginations. We do stage make-up, too, which is always fun for them and for me."

At eighty, McGrath looked back at his life and saw it as a journey, sometimes with maps on paved roads and sometimes off the map over uncharted territory. He thought back to his own childhood and saw himself with his mother, father, and Uncle Napoleon Bonaparte Bernier. He recalled Prospect Street, his own childhood street, which was unpaved, and, beyond it, the wilds on the outskirts of Tacoma.

He knew that there would never be a perfect system of education, and he didn't want one, either. "That would be terrible, if it was perfect," he said. "Then we wouldn't have to struggle; we wouldn't have angst or ecstasy. Struggling is what humanity is about."

CHAPTER TEN

To Teach Is to Love Again: Art Old and New

I. Art for the Very Old

At eight on a Thursday
morning, McGrath drove from his home to Ponce de
Leon Retirement Center in Santa Fe to teach an art
class to eighty- and ninety-year-olds who arrived with
hearing aids, canes, walkers, and in wheelchairs, too,
some of them hooked up to life-giving oxygen tanks. The
art class also kept them alive and obviously happy to
be creative. The students took their places around the
tables that McGrath arranged in the center of the room.
Most were women; today there was only one man, John,
who came from New York. At eighty, James McGrath
was younger than they were. He was still an active pilgrim and still looking for new horizons.

Irene was ninety-seven and got right to work. Others
struggled with brushes, paints, and paper. They weren't
sure what to do when McGrath told them, "We're going
to Japan today." To put them in a Japanese frame of
mind, he exhibited a luxurious Japanese wedding gown

that he brought back long ago from Tokyo. He wanted the residents at the Ponce de Leon Retirement Center to pretend they were in Japan. He talked about Japanese *haiku* and played a recording of Puccini's opera *Madame Butterfly*, as well as Gagaku temple music, often heard at the start of the New Year.

One woman looked at the wedding gown and said, "I want to try to paint. I hope I can do it," to which McGrath replied, "Of course you can." A woman with arthritis had difficulty getting paint out of the tube. McGrath helped her—and others, too—but he seemed to know instinctively when to leave well enough alone and when to swoop down and offer suggestions and compliments. To Billie Morris, he said, "I think you're doing a nice job," though she replied, "I think it's good for the waste basket." She was harder on herself than anyone else was and called herself, "You stupid thing." To Irene, McGrath said, "Gorgeous colors," and to Margaret, he said, "Put more water on your brush. That will help."

172

One woman didn't want to paint anything Japanese. "I wanna do fruit," she said. McGrath told her, "Well, do that." No one was rebuked or punished, and almost everyone was encouraged, rewarded, and appreciated. The previous week, the theme for the class was hunting, appropriately enough since it was hunting season in New Mexico, and McGrath brought to class deer antlers and clay sculptures of deer. Today he displayed artwork on the walls and encouraged students to sell it or give it away to their children and grandchildren. By eleven a.m., after a few hours of creating, the students were ready to leave. They wheeled themselves out of the room and down the long corridor. "Did you learn anything about Japan today?" McGrath asked Margaret. "No," she said, and he replied, "It's definitely a different culture."

McGrath began to clean up. He wiped the paint from plastic tablecloths, dried them, and folded them. It had been a good class, and he was happy despite the negative voices he'd heard.

"I like the way they react to and with each other," he said. "They trust one another. They're all aware of what the others in the class are doing, though some seem to be focused only on what's right in front of them. They usually figure out how to solve their own creative problems. I rarely make suggestions. In many ways, teaching older people is not that different from teaching young kids, and that's not a criticism."

Laurie McGrath, the lifestyle program director at Ponce de Leon and no relation to James, appreciated what he did. "He offers our residents opportunities to feel pride," she said. "He gives them a voice. As someone who has studied aging and who works with older adults, I can say that this is probably the greatest gift he brings to them."

173

II. Art for the Very Young

It was the middle of July. On a morning before the sun scorched the earth, McGrath set out from home for the Hopi reservation in Arizona with a suitcase, a box of art supplies, and gallons of water. The Hopi reservation in Hotevilla is almost directly west of Santa Fe. McGrath took Route 40, then 191 to 264, and west again. He went over rough terrain, skirting most of the tourist landmarks, such as the Painted Desert.

"I know the route by heart," he said. "I feel I could drive blindfolded." It's four hundred miles or so to Hotevilla and takes about six hours of steady driving to get

there. Ever since the early 1960s, McGrath has traveled there. At first, he went with Charles and Otellie
Loloma when they were married to one another. Then,
after they separated and divorced — and after Charles
returned to the reservation in 1965 — Otellie and James
made the journey together. The road helped to fuse
them together into a couple. In fact, Otellie trusted
him well enough to tell him Hopi stories that she had
heard from family members and that were rarely if ever
shared with outsiders.

"My relationship with Otellie was the most deeply
spiritual relationship in my whole life," McGrath remembered. "I would say that there was a great deal of trust
between us."

For many years, when he visited Hotevilla, he stayed
with Otellie in her ancient house of stone and mud that
sat on the edge of the mesa. She took him into the Hopi
world, introduced him to the Hopi *kivas*, the underground rooms that are entered from above by ladders
and used for religious ceremonies. Jim and Otellie also
observed Hopi women make *piki*, a wafer-thin bread,
using blue corn meal, finely powdered ashes, and a pinch
of salt. Of course, he tasted *piki* and grew to like it. He
learned Hopi words and knew, too, that males had a different language than females. "*Kakwah* is the word that
males use to say 'thank you,'" he explained. "*Esquawli* is
the word females use."

McGrath learned the Hopi language and culture
by watching, listening, and teaching on the reservation — not by studying in a library. His main teacher
was Otellie, who was born in Sipaulovi Village, grew up
on the reservation, and belonged to the Sun clan. Her
Hopi name, which she rarely if ever used in the Anglo
world, was "Sequafnema." As a token of her trust for

McGrath, she allowed him to use it in the title of his portrait of her — a stunning work that feels as though it's infused with his love for her.

The main thing that he learned from Otellie and Charles Loloma was, he explained, that the Hopi don't "teach" in the contemporary American and European sense of the word. "Otellie and Charles never lectured," he said. "They took me to dances, told stories, and shared food. They never said, 'Listen to me now,' 'Listen to this,' or 'I want to teach you something.' They instructed me in much the same way that my Chehalis uncle, Napoleon Bonaparte Bernier, taught me when I was a boy in the State of Washington. They took me on walks and showed me things, like where to find wild honey and where to dig for clams."

In the early 1970s and for many years thereafter, McGrath taught at the Hopi school that was under the auspices of the Bureau of Indian Affairs. Years later, he began to teach at Hopitutukaiki, a small private non-profit school funded by the World in Harmony Foundation, founded in 2005 by Robert Rhodes, an Anglo who was married to Verma Nequatewa, Charles Loloma's niece and a renowned Hopi artist. Rhodes's original idea was to "develop and implement a school for Hopi students based in Hopi philosophy."

What alarmed him, perhaps more than anything else, was the fact that proportionally more Indians dropped out of schools than the members of any other group in America. It seemed to Rhodes that the main reason Indians did not graduate from school was because the educational system was "imposed on them." That system, he explained, was developed from a "European model and filtered through mainstream American development and culture." Rhodes wanted a school that would be thoroughly Hopi and that would use "local resources, philosophy, and teaching."

In his school, teachers were required to attend Hopi ceremonies "as appropriate and as allowed." They were required to make home visits, meet with parents, understand and appreciate home environments. Moreover, parents were welcomed in the school "at all times, so long as their presence increased student learning." Rhodes expected the parents and the community to participate actively in the educational process. Perhaps his most unorthodox concept was that "school may take place anyplace that is appropriate." Indeed, he wanted "school outside of school," as he put it. He believed that Hopi students could and would learn without the aid of a teacher and on ranches, in fields, and in their own homes.

176

McGrath met Bob Rhodes in Hotevilla, where he was teaching music, and, over the years, they became friends and colleagues. McGrath liked his ideas immensely. He had always believed strongly in field trips and he knew, too, from his own experience, that learning often takes place outside of school and when teachers are not present. Hopitutukaiki was a perfect place for McGrath to teach art—or not to teach it, as the case may be. At Hopitutukaiki, he would "facilitate learning," as he phrased it.

"I would say that I share skills and insights rather than teach," McGrath explained. "Teaching implies putting something into somebody, and I don't do that on the Hopi reservation."

The fact that there was no actual schoolhouse in Hotevilla also appealed to McGrath; he had been teaching students in and out of schools and in and out of classrooms since 1952. At Hotevilla, he shared his skills. His life there and his work there were almost as one and indivisible. He woke early, performed his morning rituals, dressed, and walked across the highway to have breakfast with Rhodes. Over bacon, eggs, toast, and fresh fruit, they talked about the day ahead. Bob wanted the students to use both Hopi and English words, and he and McGrath discussed ways to make that happen. Now, it was time to move on. At about 8:00 a.m., students began to arrive by themselves and in groups of two and three. Some came on foot, walking across fields where corn, beans, and squash grew. Others arrived by car. There were young people—both boys and girls—and older people. The age range was from about six to forty.

McGrath had taught Hopi families for so long that former students were now grandparents. A father or a mother would come into the classroom with a son or a daughter and ask McGrath if he remembered their name and recognized their face. Of course he did, and he invited grandmothers and their grandchildren to sit together and make art side-by-side.

"The young ones are especially enthusiastic, though at first they are shy and quiet," McGrath said. "They soon become trusting, and they chatter away. If they are returning from a previous class, they sometimes call me Jim. Otherwise I'm Mr. McGrath. Of course, they're well aware that I'm an Anglo and an outsider, but that doesn't seem to create a barrier. We get to know one another little-by-little. On the first day, they introduce themselves. We go around the room, and the students give their first and their last names. In the class that I call 'Fun With Clay,' I remember Dante Dallas, Taylor Seechoma, June Honhongva, Gretta Quotskuuva, Alicia Nequatewa, and Mikaela Garcia."

In the writing classes for the Hopi students, McGrath begins by asking about the writing they see around them. At first they're usually unsure what he means or where he wants to go with his strange questions. There's silence in the room. Then he asks, "Are there things in nature that tell us stories?" Now the Hopi students catch on. "Plants and animals tell stories," one girl says. McGrath follows his first question with another and another after that one; as usual, he asks lots of questions. "How do animals tell stories?" he wants to know. A boy says, "They leave markings," and McGrath asks, "What kinds of markings?" Now the class is animated. "Footprints!" several students shout at the same time.

They're itching to go outside. They take their sketchbooks and look for writings in nature. A boy notices a beetle making marks as it moves. A stray dog wanders about, leaves signs, and then, too, there are ripples that the wind has made in the sand. The students notice everything. The assignment that McGrath gives them is

to create six different sketches of animals and insects, and they're soon hard at work. While they draw in their notebooks, an older woman wanders into the group, asks "what are you doing," and joins them. She sees a lizard, points to it, and the lizard enters their artwork. The students bring their notebooks inside, eager to use their images and ideas. McGrath asks them to write a story, a song, or a poem about a dog, a beetle, or a lizard. "Make it up," he says. The work is supposed to include both words and pictures and to make something that's bigger than words and pictures alone.

In another class that McGrath teaches, the students make shields with canvas that they stretch across aluminum rings. They create their own colors—reds, purples, oranges, greens, and blues—from the environment around them. McGrath asks the students to tell him the Hopi word for "color" and the words for the specific colors that appear in their work; he encourages them to use both Hopi and English words. Then he shows them how to make smooth pigments that have the consistency of milk; he also shows them that smaller brushes can be used effectively to convey details while larger brushes work better for big, broad strokes.

Furthermore, McGrath invites the students to make their own pictures of the world that they see everyday all around them: farmers' cornfields, rocks, the dry arroyos, and the gentle hills. Sometimes he suggests that they make a painting from a bug's or a lizard's point of view. After days of work—or is it play?—the students share their creations. McGrath selects art and displays it on the wall. There's an instant exhibit for the whole community to see and to appreciate.

"Parents come by and make positive comments," McGrath says. "That provides real encouragement for the students."

At the end of the day, McGrath cleans up the studio. Then he walks home and joins Bob, Verma, and their family for grilled steak, boiled corn from the fields, squash with a local herb called *na-na-gof-see*, and Hopi iced tea, *ho-ho-see*. They talk about the day's events, watch the moon rise in the sky, and wash dishes together. McGrath walks home, gets ready for bed, and before falling asleep thinks about the next day's class.

III. No Time Not to Love

Robert Rhodes is proud of what he and McGrath have achieved at the Hopi School and proud of its influence on the community. But Rhodes is also alarmed by the signs of cultural change that he sees, especially by what he calls "the erosion of Hopi culture."

"There's a resistance to preserving the old ways and many people here think that education is sitting in a classroom, writing on the blackboard, and taking a test," he said. "They don't see our arts program as real education and that's sad."

Rhodes has a long history of working with Indians on their own turf. He has a long perspective that provides him with a sense of big historical transformations. Born in Indiana and raised in Arizona, Rhodes taught at Arizona State University and Northern Arizona University. Over the course of many years, he has watched as "the dominant culture eroded the values of the Hopi people." Still he doesn't give up. He believes strongly in the Hopi philosophy of education that takes a holistic approach to learning and emphasizes the connections between art and culture.

180

"McGrath has played an important role in our program," he said. "He doesn't tell people what to do. They find whatever they need to find in themselves, and they stretch themselves, too. To my way of thinking, that's more valuable than memorizing and taking exams."

When Rhodes's wife, Verma, published a book about her own work as a jeweler, she asked McGrath to write a foreword and to provide some of his own poetry. In "I Sing With My Fingers," he expresses the view of creativity that he learned from her uncle, Charles Loloma, who said

> *I feel the stone and think*
> *Not to conquer it,*
> *But to help it express itself.*

Going to Hoteville is always a bittersweet experience for McGrath and an adventure that takes him to the brink of a new world of learning. "It's one of the strangest places I have ever known," he says. "It's stranger than Yemen, Korea, or the Philippines. When I go there, I'm reminded of my days with Otellie Loloma." He pauses a moment, looks at the magpies outside his window, and then continues.

"Otellie and I were both aware of the boundaries between us, and we didn't want to violate them or to use one another," he says. "We were aware that we came from and lived in very different cultures. Still we crossed boundaries, worked together, made art together, and taught together. We learned whole universes from one another."

McGrath remembers the time when he wanted to see her more than anything else. "I drove to her village," he says. "It was late at night. The house was locked, but I was so eager that I broke in through the bathroom window."

Teachers aren't supposed to break into houses, even the houses of those they love. McGrath has always emphasized love and insisted that teachers ought to love their students, knowing full well that the word "love" has lost much of its meaning today. Indeed, in a world in which students learn to love hamburgers, fries, new jeans, and cell phones, they often don't appreciate the deeper meanings of love.

"We are creatures that need love," McGrath says. "We need it no matter what age we are. Teachers need it and want it. Students need it and want it, too. There's really no time not to love." Then, to make sure that his meaning comes across, he adds, "Love is sharing what's important: time, dreams, and experiences. To teach is to love again."

At home, he began to give away many of the worldly possessions he had gathered from around the world, beginning in the 1950s and continuing for the next six decades. His things had turned the house into a kind of living museum. Parts of his vast collection of art went to the Smithsonian in Washington, D.C., and parts to museums in Washington State. He was simplifying his life again, and the process of unburdening made him feel a whole lot lighter. He had less to carry around with him and less to worry about.

"I do feel guilty loading people up with treasures," he said. "But letting go of possessions seems like the right thing to do at this stage of my life." Not surprisingly, it was much harder to let go of friends such as Mary Lou Denning. During the last year of her life, James visited Mary Lou in the hospital sometimes once a week, sometimes more. "We remembered our days together in Europe when World War II was not long over, and then the stormy years at the IAIA when history itself seemed to change and American Indians rose up to claim their rightful inheritance. Mary Lou and I listened to music together and read poetry. We were close until the end. I can hardly believe she's gone, though I know it's true. I have so many memories. I don't know how I'll ever give all of them away."

Ten Quotations
from James McGrath

1. "Art is a world to explore, create, and recreate."

2. "Make your life beautiful and keep it moving."

3. "Discover who you are."

4. "Practice awareness and humility."

5. "Share your freedom and expression with others."

6. "Take risks and create space for risks to happen."

7. "Be connected to all."

8. "Sometimes it's better to be David than Goliath."

9. "Operate under the Behemoth.

10. "To teach is to love again."

Acknowledgments

There is hardly a part of McGrath's life I have not asked him about and that he has not shared with me. Looking back at our conversations, I would say that little by little we went deeper and deeper into his art and teaching, as though peeling away the layers of an onion. McGrath didn't reveal everything about himself all at once, but in stages. We learned to trust one another—an essential element if you are going to write a book about someone who is alive and whose cooperation you want and need. I also conducted research at McGrath's archives in the Special Collections at the University of Washington in Seattle, where he was a student in the 1950s. Carla Rickerson, the head of Special Collections, assisted my search for McGrath materials. In addition, I used the archives at IAIA in Santa Fe. IAIA's archivist Ryan Flahive found all the information I wanted, needed, and more. I have quoted here from Winona Garmhausen's interview with the artist, Fritz Scholder, and have permission to do so. The citation is MS07. Garmhausen Papers. Box 4, Folder 7, Archives of IAIA.

I burrowed into McGrath's own personal archives at his house in Santa Fe. Fortunately he saved almost everything pertaining to his own education and teaching—more than seventy years of documents. At Sonoma State University, Jack Ritchie was once again a major help. Also at SSU John Muller found hard-to-find films and showed them to me in the library. Professor Michael Schwager in the SSU art department read and made valuable comments about the sections of this book on Bill Allan, William Wiley, and Bob Hudson. Professor Les Adler in the Hutchins School at SSU read the chapter about Richland during the Cold War and provided useful suggestions and insights. SSU Professor Greg Sarris, the tribal chairman of the Graton Rancheria, read the chapters about McGrath's years at IAIA and gave me the benefit of his own experiences among the Indians of California and his own years of scholarship. Ellen Meyers—who has devoted her lifetime to teaching and learning—read this book closely and made detailed comments, and thus helped to make it stronger, tighter.

To write this book, I drew upon my own experiences as a teacher. I discussed the project as I was writing it with fellow teachers at SSU and around the country as well as friends and family, including my brother Daniel, who was a teacher for decades, and my sister-in-law Adelina Aramburo, who has been a school principal in San Francisco.

I want to thank all the people who talked to me about McGrath—nearly forty individuals including Bill Allan, Thomas Bier, Alfred Clah, Nansi Bainard,

Aida Mankowski Davis, Mary Lou Denning, Jack Di Benedetto, Tom Drysdale, Earl Eder, John Haugse, Bob Hudson, Jeanette Katoney, Irene Oliver-Lewis, Phil McCracken, Laurie McGrath, Veronica Orr, Christine Taylor Patten, Julie Reid, Robert Rhodes, Joan Rudholm, Tom Rudholm, Beth Rudolph, Yvonne Schack, Karen Schlesinger, Corneila Schulz, Jim Scoggin, Kevin Red Star, Betty Taira, Violet Hunter Vaughnes, Jeni Viney, Dorothy Wiley, William Wiley, and Bill Witherup. I also benefited from conversations with Robert Hayden, Jon Quam, Mark Heydon, and Peter Selz, who welcomed me to his house in Berkeley and showed me his amazing art collection. Cornelia Schulz shared her memories of Bob Hudson and her experiences as a painter and an art teacher.

I consulted with Professor John Kornfeld at Sonoma State University; Professor Pedro Noguera at New York University; and Professor David Stoloff at Eastern Connecticut State University. Chip McAuley was a reader I could count on for good advice. Michael Morey caught many typos. I extend my gratitude to all of the many students I have known, especially those in the First Year Experience classes—the pilgrims to the horizon—who taught me in my last years of teaching what I ought to have known when I began to teach nearly half a century ago.

James Retherford turned my manuscript into a real work of art, which is fitting given the fact that *In A Class By Himself* is about an art teacher and an artist. An artistic book seems to be a good way to honor McGrath, his students, and fellow teachers.

Bibliography

Ablon, Joan. "The American Indian Chicago Conference." *Journal of American Indian Education*, January, 1962.

Abram, David. *The Spell of the Sensuous: Perception and Language in a More-Than-Human World*. New York: Vintage, 1997. Originally published 1996.

Arendt, Hannah. "The Crisis in Education," collected in *Between Past and Future: Eight Exercises in Political Thought*. New York: Viking, 1968.

Astrov, Margot, edited and with an introductory essay. *The Winged Spirit: An Anthology of American Indian Prose and Poetry*. New York: Capricorn, 1962. Originally published 1946.

Awiakata, Marilou. *Selu: Seeking the Corn-Mother's Wisdom*. Golden, Colorado: Fulcrum, 1993.

Ayers, William. *A Simple Justice: The Challenge of Small Schools*. New York: Teachers College Press, 2000.

Bannon, Laura. *Mind Your Child's Art: A Guide for Parents and Teachers.* New York: Pellegrini & Cudahy, 1952.

Brandon, William. *The American Heritage Book of Indians.* Introduction by John F. Kennedy. New York: Dell, 1961.

Boyce, George. *When Navajos Had Too Many Sheep: the 1940s.* San Francisco: Indian Historian Press, 1974.

Cheshire, Maxine. "Braves Stage Pow-Wow for VIPs." *The Washington Post.* March 30, 1965.

Coates, Robert M. "Our Far-Flung Correspondents: Indian Affairs, New Style." *The New Yorker.* June 17, 1967.

"Create What You Know! McGrath Teaches Art from the Roots." *Pasatiempo Magazine.* Nov. 14, 1995.

Cutter, John A. "Creativity and Aging." *Mature Outlook.* Feb. 2001.

Csikszentmihalyi, Mihaly. *Flow: The Psychology of Optimal Experience.* New York: Harper Perennial, 1990.

Darling-Hammond, Linda, Letitia Fickel, Julia Koppich, and others. *Powerful Teacher Education: Lessons from Exemplary Programs.* San Francisco: Jossey-Bass, 2006.

_____. *The Right to Learn: A Blue Print for Creating Schools That Work.* San Francisco: Jossey-Bass, 1997.

Davis, Jessica Hoffmann. *Why Our Schools Need the Arts.* New York: Teachers College, 2008.

Diamond, Julie. *Welcome to the Aquarium: A Year in the Lives of Children.* Foreword by Jules Feiffer. New York: New Press, 2008.

Finch, L. Boyd. *Legacies of Camelot: Stewart and Lee Udall: American Culture, and the Arts.* Foreword by

Tom Udall. Norman: University of Oklahoma, 2008.

Freire, Paulo. *Pedagogy of the Oppressed*. New York: Herder, 1970. Originally published 1968.

Garmhausen, Winona. *History of Indian Arts Education in Santa Fe: the Institute of American Indian Arts*. Santa Fe: Sunstone, 1988.

Giroux, Henry A. *Pedagogy and the Politics of Hope: Theory, Culture, and Schooling*. Boulder: Westview, 1997.

Gladwell, Malcolm. "Most Likely to Succeed." *The New Yorker*, December 15, 2008, 36-42.

_____. The Tipping Point: *How Little Things Can Make a Big Difference*. Boston: Little, Brown, 2000.

Gritton, Joy L. *The Institute of American Indian Arts: Modernism and U.S. Indian Policy*. Albuquerque: University of New Mexico, 2000.

_____. "Cross-Cultural Education vs. Modernist Imperialism: The Institute of American Indian Arts." *Art Journal*, Autumn, 1992.

Highwater, Jamake. "My Reservations About That Indian Series." *The New York Times*, Aug. 8, 1976.

Illich, Ivan. *Deschooling Society*. New York: Harper & Row, 1971.

Kidder, Tracy. *Among School Children*. Boston: Houghton Mifflin, 1989.

Kozloff, Max. "West Coast Art: Vital Pathology." *The Nation*, Aug. 24, 1964.

Kuhn, Jill A., ed. *In Cabin Six: An Anthology of Poetry by Male Survivors of Sexual Abuse*. Big Bear City, CA.: Impact, 2000.

LaRiviere, Anne L. "New Art By the Oldest Americans." *Westways*, May, 1973.

Loeb, Paul. *Nuclear Culture: Living and Working in the World's Largest Atomic Complex*. New York: Coward, McCann & Geoghegan,1982.

Lowenfeld, Viktor. *Your Child and His Art*. New York: Macmillan, 1954.

McGrath, James. "Uncle Nap." *Man!*

_____ with Mary Lou Denning. *Art and Indian Children*. Washington, D.C.: Department of the Interior, 1970.

_____. *Dance with Indian Children: The Shape of the Drum Beat, the Rattle Sound, the Flute Voice*. Washington: Center for the Arts of Indian America, 1972.

_____. *Future Directions in Native American Art*. Santa Fe: Institute of American Indian Arts, 1972.

_____ with Louis Ballard. *My Music Reaches to the Sky: Native American Musical Instruments*. Washington, D.C.: Center for the Arts of Indian America, 1973.

_____. *At the Edgelessness of Light*. Santa Fe: Sunstone, 2005.

_____. *Speaking with Magpies*. Santa Fe: Sunstone, 2007

_____. *Dreaming Invisible Voices*. Santa Fe: Sunstone, 2009.

_____, co-author and co-producer. *Two Indians: Red Reflections on Life*, a twenty-six-minute 16mm color documentary. Centron Educational Films.

Mathews, Jay. *Class Struggle: What's Wrong (and Right) With America's Best Public High Schools*. New York: Times Books, 1998.

Momaday, N. Scott. *The Man Made of Words: Essays, Stories, Passages*. New York: St. Martin's Press, 1997.

Neuberger, Richard L. "What's a Treaty With an Indian Worth?" *Christian Herald*, Aug. 1953.

Nelson, Jacqueline. "White on the Outside, but Red on

the Inside." *The Santa Fe New Mexican*, May 12, 1973.

Noguera, Pedro. *City Schools and the American Dream: Reclaiming the Promise of Public Education*. New York: Teachers College Press, 2003.

Page, Susanne and Jake Page. *Hopi*. New York: Abrams, 1982.

Perreault, John. "Metaphysical Funk Monk." *ARTnews*, May 1968.

Ravitch, Diane. *The Troubled Crusade: American Education, 1945-1980*. New York: Basic Books, 1983.

Read, Herbert. *The Grass Roots of Art: Lectures on the Social Aspects of Art in an Industrial Age*. New York: George Wittenborn, 1955. Originally published 1946.

Reese, William J. *America's Public Schools: From the Common School to "No Child Left Behind."* Baltimore: Johns Hopkins, 2005.

Richman, Robin. "100 Years Later, a Double Rediscovery." *Life*, Dec. 1, 1967.

Robert Hudson: *The Sonoma County Years, 1977-2005*. Santa Rosa: Sonoma County Museum, 2005.

Rose, Mike. *Lives on the Boundary: A Moving Account of the Struggles and Achievements of America's Educationally Underprepared*. New York: Penguin, 1990. Originally published 1989.

Schmitz, Tony. "Film Makers' Reflections." *Arizona Highways*. August, 1976.

Selz, Peter. *Art in a Turbulent Era*. Ann Arbor: Umi Research, 1985.

Stevens, Elizabeth. "Pop & Op Seep Into Indians' Artistry. *The Washington Post*, April 25, 1965.

Stiles, Kristine and Peter Selz. *Theories and Documents of Contemporary Art: A Sourcebook of Artists'*

Writings. Berkeley: University of California Press, 1996.

Taubman, Howard. "Indians in Santa Fe," a two-part series. *The New York Times*, May 16 and May 18, 1967.

Transient Poet: William Allan Retrospective. Sacramento: Crocker Art Museum, 1993.

Tyack, David B. *The One Best System: A History of American Urban Education*. Cambridge: Harvard, 1974.

U.S. Department of Education. *A Nation At Risk: The Imperative for Educational Reform*. Washington, D.C., 1983.

White, Richard. *The Organic Machine: The Remaking of the Columbia River*. New York: Hill and Wang, 1995.

192 William Wiley: *Selections from Two Exhibitions, New York and San Francisco: John Berggruen and Charles Cowles Galleries*, 2007.

Witherup, Bill. *Men at Work*. Boise: Boise State, 1989.

_____. *Down Wind, Down River*. Albuquerque: West End Press, 2000.